COMING OUT OF THE FIRE

Bishop Roscoe Williams

Copyright © 2023 Roscoe Williams

ALL RIGHTS RESERVED. This book contains material protected under International and Federal Copyright Laws and Treaties. Any unauthorized reprint or use of this material is prohibited. No part of this book may be reproduced or transmitted in any form or by any means, electronic or mechanical, including photocopying, recording, or by any information storage and retrieval system without express written permission from the author/publisher.

Some names and identifying details have been changed
to protect the privacy of individuals.

Scripture quotations are from the Holy Bible, New Living Translation, copyright © 1996, 2004, 2015 by Tyndale House Foundation. Used by permission of Tyndale House Publishers, Carol Stream, Illinois 60188, USA. All rights reserved.

Scripture quotations are from the King James Version of the Bible. All rights reserved.

Scripture quotations are from the Holy Bible, New International Version®, NIV®. Copyright ©1973, 1978, 1984, 2011 by Biblica, Inc.™ Used by permission of Zondervan. All rights reserved worldwide. www.zondervan.com The "NIV" and "New International Version" are trademarks registered in the United States Patent and Trademark Office by Biblica, Inc.™

Scripture quotations are from the ESV® Bible (The Holy Bible, English Standard Version®), copyright © 2001 by Crossway, a publishing ministry of Good News Publishers. Used by permission. All rights reserved.

Book Cover Design: Prize Publishing House

Printed by: Prize Publishing House, LLC in the United States of America.

First printing edition 2023.

Prize Publishing House
P.O. Box 9856, Chesapeake, VA 23321
www.PrizePublishingHouse.com

Library of Congress Control Number: 2023910368

ISBN (Hardcover): 979-8-9884324-4-9
ISBN (E-Book): 979-8-9884324-5-6

Table of Contents

Dedication v

Foreword vii

Chapter 1: Baba Black Sheep 1

Chapter 2: When Desperation Is All You Have 7

Chapter 3: Military Man 17

Chapter 4: War Zone 23

Chapter 5: End Of An Era 29

Chapter 6: He Came To See About Me 37

Chapter 7: Miracles, Signs, and Wonders 51

Chapter 8: If I Could Just Tell My Story 75

Dedication

First and foremost, I dedicate this book to my Lord and Savior, Jesus Christ, who has given me the grace and mercy to tell of all the goodness He has shown me.

Secondly, to my wonderful and lovely wife, Vickie (Teresa) Williams, who has stood with me and supported me throughout our relationship before marriage and in marriage for over 40 years; a constant support and patient wife who has never stopped loving me no matter what. God bless you, sweetheart.

To my three children, Andre Williams, Shaneri Nash (Williams), and Kermitrice Williams, whom God gifted to me. You have assisted me in the ministry since I started this journey 25 years ago. You sacrificed your lives and your jobs for the Kingdom of God, keeping our businesses and church thriving because "we are family."

I also send my love and thank you to my family, Eric, Nia, Ethan, and Nydia. I love you with all my heart.

AOFC Family Church, thank you for supporting and putting up with me as your pastor and trusting me in every situation.

To my father and mother, who instilled in me the right things, to always put God first and to stay with God.

To my siblings who helped me grow up in life and kept me happy and laughing, James Harper (deceased), Joyce Hunter (deceased), Bobby Williams, Herbert Williams (deceased), Ever Richardson, Karlene Sneed (my devoted sister), Melvin Williams, Johnny Williams (deceased), Ruby Fite Williams, and Barbara Dixon.

To my good friend, Prophet Sylvester Walker (deceased), who always told me to "write a book of your testimonies."

To Prophetess Janice Mixon, who inspired me to use my gift with this book, and Cedric and Candance, who knew just how to say what I wanted to say and made this book possible.

To the many relatives, friends, and associates that if I tried to mention, room would not allow.

May every reader be touched and inspired by this book, and may God bless you in the hour of temptation as He has kept me. May God's love abound in you. God Bless.

—Bishop Roscoe Williams

Foreword

In the fall of 1981, two young but devoted people driven by a divine vision started a church called Calvary Temple Apostolic Church in Dallas, Texas. The church was born from a prayer meeting of 10 people (including babies) who met at the couple's home. That September, they held their first service. Filled with expectations and armed with the Word of God, the leaders had little resources and few members.

A good friend, called Pastor Clifford L. and Pamela J. Frazier, recommending a Longview family, who was now living in Dallas, they should minister to. This was Frazier's first evangelistic opportunity. Immediately, they scheduled a series of Bible studies at the Williams' home. Each week, the Williams family eagerly and faithfully attended the classes. The Fraziers were excited because their meetings were about as close as many adults came to being part of the church.

One of those classes lasted until almost midnight. I, Clifford L. Frazier, looked at the wall clock and told the family that the clock read about 15 minutes to midnight. However, on God's clock, it was only a few minutes to midnight. Roscoe Williams jumped up abruptly and said, "I want to be baptized!" Then his brother, John Williams, jumped up, declaring he wanted to get baptized, too. I had never seen two brothers arguing over who would be baptized first!

That was the beginning of a great evangelistic thrust for the fledgling church. Seven adult members of the Williams family got saved and joined the church. They proved to be an extremely faithful family whom we counted on as the church grew. And it did.

The Williams family played a significant part in every phase of the church's development. One of the family members felt a call to the ministry. Over the intervening years, he advanced from a young minister to one of three associate pastors of the church, leading the church's evangelistic ministry. Entire campaigns focused on seven or eight neighborhoods surrounding the church were overseen by this faithful minister, Roscoe Williams. Over the intervening years, many souls were added to the church, prompting Calvary to move to larger facilities three times.

In 1997, Roscoe Williams was invited to assume the role of pastor at a different church. He initially declined the offer, citing that he was needed and too busy at his home church to take on the assignment; however, he did tell me about the offer. I said to him that while I very much depended upon his service to our church, he shouldn't say no to the opportunity. "You never know what God might be doing," I advised.

Reluctantly, but with my blessing, Elder Roscoe Williams and his family went to serve what is now the Alpha and Omega Ministries Church. It would be wrong for me to tell more of his story. Instead, prepare yourself to be enlightened, inspired, and possibly in awe as you read the story of the now Bishop Roscoe Williams and his wife, Co-Pastor Vicki Williams, along with his children, Andre, Shaneri, and Kermitrice, who grew up in the church. I believe that you will be blessed as you do!

Yours because of Calvary,

Bishop Clifford L. Frazier
Founding Pastor of HeartLine Ministries
Chief Prelate of Ho Logos Fellowship of Churches

CHAPTER One

Baba Black Sheep

"I knew you before I formed you in your mother's womb. Before you were born I set you apart and appointed you as my prophet to the nations."

~ Jeremiah 1:5, NLT

The black sheep is the darkest one in the family. Sometimes shunned, often ridiculed…rarely celebrated. That was me – *the black sheep*. Of course, *black sheep* isn't a formal title. Neither is it earned, but it's quietly understood. Those small nuances are in the way the "least of the sheep" are spoken to. The quiet, negative connotations and passive placement on the family tree unintentionally take precedence over making every branch feel equal. Even though it isn't done on purpose, the treatment of the *black sheep* has lasting effects that linger in the air, like the scent of a candle long after it has stopped burning.

Have you ever felt like the *black sheep*? Ever wonder why?

My grandmother nicknamed me *Shine*. Growing up, I hadn't considered what that name really meant. Many years would pass before a friend of mine from church would relay the truth about the moniker I'd inherited from my grandmother. "Hold him up so I can see him," she told the midwife who helped birth me. Once she laid eyes on me, my grandmother spoke my purpose right then and there, "Shine," she prophesied over me. "He's going to be the preacher in the family."

Despite the powerful name I'd been given growing up, my skin made me feel a different way about myself like I was separated. "Why am I so dark-skinned?" I asked God. Unfortunately, I never heard the answer. So, I went on about my days, wondering why the stigma of my skin made things so different for me. Being the seventh of eleven children (six boys, five girls), it was hard being expected to get food for the family and walking my mother to work. Still, those responsibilities were stacked on my shoulders. And no one cared except me…and my dark skin.

The City of Longview, East Texas

I may have been the *black sheep*, but I always knew there was something unique about me. Let me clarify here: I grew up in a very loving family. My formative years were spent in Longview, Texas, about 127 miles outside of Dallas. My father worked for a company called Lone Star Steel, and my mother was a housewife, which I relay with the utmost respect and pride. My family stayed in church; Pentecostal raised, to be exact. *Bethel Temple of Longview. Wow, there are so many memories there.* My parents ensured we were members in good standing, and my grandparents, Deacon Hezekiah and Lee Johnigan, were esteemed members of the flock. My elders were highly influential in my becoming engrained not only in the church but in the Body of Christ. This would all serve my best interest years later; as the Bible declares, it all worked together for my good.

We had a wonderful time growing up, but make no mistake – there were many difficult times, too. As my father grew older, his health declined. At the time, Lone Star Steel required that all employees pass annual physicals. Unfortunately, my father suffered from hypertension, which the doctors didn't know how to treat. Consequently, he was laid off, catapulting our family into a pit we weren't prepared for.

In the midst of turmoil, I remember still going to church, sitting on the front pew, staring at our pastor, Elder Timothy Younger, with wide-eyed wonder. As he preached, Pastor Younger ventured over to me, casually laying his hand on top of my head. "Lord, bless Brother Roscoe," he'd say. He often did that – speaking blessings over me as I observed him. At the time, the small blessings didn't seem so significant. Not to the young boy that I was. However, as I matured, I came to understand that Pastor Younger was planting seeds in my life that were growing me in the spirit. Thinking back, I now see how unique our relationship was, just like my bond with my parents. Initially, they assigned me what I thought to be menial chores meant for the *black sheep* since their other children were too precious. These days, I've realized that certain tasks my parents asked me to do showed the love they genuinely had for their *number seven*.

Why do I always have to be the one to shave you? I used to wonder as my father asked me to shave his face. *Out of 11 kids, you want me to be the shaver?* Of course, I never voiced my thoughts to my father; I just went on and did as he asked, taking his old razor and making sure he looked good. On the other hand, my mother had to go to work since my father could not. Guess who she'd wake up to walk her to work at 4:00 a.m.? Me, of course! We made our way through the old graveyard, and I put on a brave face for my mother, but on the inside...I was scared! I felt alone, but as we navigated through the dark terrains, there was a tug pulling at me that I couldn't shake. Of all her boys, why had my mother appointed me her guardian to get where she needed to go? There had to be a reason. Back then, I was unaware, but the answer to why she and my father depended so heavily on me to help follow through on certain aspects of their lives was because God had such an incredible purpose for me.

The *black sheep* wasn't being mistreated after all. It wasn't outwardly apparent; however, I was *preferred*. Even my teachers saw something special in me and weren't afraid to let me or anyone else know it. "There's something special about you," they'd say. "One day, you're going to grow up to be something big!" Now some teachers thought I would be a clown (I can laugh about that now), and others thought I'd grow up to be a preacher. You never know how God's directing your life. None of us truly knew where I was headed, but even at a young age, I was fully aware that God was ordering my steps; His purpose for my life just had to be revealed.

I'll never forget how my paternal grandmother helped our

family after we fell on hard times, as well as my maternal grandmother. "Go pick up some food from your grandmother," my mother instructed as she pushed me out the door to make yet another solo trip to my father's mother's house. *Here we go again,* I thought as I stepped off our porch and headed to the south side alone. Keep in mind, these were harsh times I came up in – discrimination, hostility, and violence against people of color. And there I was, a little boy trying his best to be brave as my feet stomped across the dirt roads and pavement. Ten miles later, I'd reach my grandmother's house, asking for food. Without hesitation, grandmother loaded up some bags and put me in a taxi so I could get back home.

All these experiences were pivotal in my becoming the man I am today. Without each and every one of them, I may not have discovered my destiny.

CHAPTER

Two

When Desperation Is All You Have

"We can make our plans, but the Lord determines our steps."

~ Proverbs 16:9, NLT

When I was in fifth grade, my father's death leveled my family.

Each of us children were obviously shattered, but I think my father's death traumatized my mother the most. How was she going to take care of all her children alone? How was she to go on when the love of her life was suddenly taken from her? What was her place in the world now? Earning $30 a week as a dishwasher and having to stretch it to take care of us was a burden that was too big for my mother to bear. Fueled by a nervous breakdown, she eventually had a stroke, leaving her unable to function. Our world immediately crumbled. Left without a father, it was up to my older brothers and sisters, who had scattered around various parts of East Texas and Dallas, to help pick up the load where our parents had left off.

While our younger two sisters were placed with our maternal grandmother, we ended up living with our older brothers, basically learning how to take care of ourselves. We had to use the lessons taught to us by our father to grow into the potential of who we could be. Purpose is a scary thing when you're young, especially when it seems so much bigger than you. Keep in mind, I was growing up in the 60s – the Vietnam era. The Vietnam War had taken control of the country; our young, black men were being drafted to their deaths, left and right. Families were being destroyed, and the hope of our country was dwindling to dust.

Outside of political struggles, poverty was prevalent here at home. Back then, we didn't have Medicare or Medicaid, but at least there was WIC to help those qualified to receive it. The lack of jobs for able-bodied, young Black men wanting to work were scarce. We were told not to be lazy and help ourselves, only to be slapped in the face with rejection after rejection when it came to making a decent living. We weren't trying to get rich; we were desperate to LIVE. We'd get out of school with nothing to do for the summer, so we had to find something to keep us out of trouble. With nothing to keep me busy at home, life took a turn that it wouldn't have taken had I been involved in something constructive. I found myself getting involved with the wrong people…and the wrong things.

I'll never forget my friends and me pulling together with the bright idea to start a gang on our side of town. Once I picked up the gang, I also started picking up bad habits. We started experimenting with drugs. Back then, we were given matchboxes of "marijuana." That's what we called the little $2-3 hits we bought. We also dabbled in drinking syrup and alcohol, too. My father wasn't around any longer to encourage me, my mother was sick, and my brothers were drinking and partying, just like me. I had no one to tell me I was spiraling out of control. No one was there to pull me out of the mire, lay down the law, or tell me to snap out of it. My bad habits became a comfort to me, a security blanket of sorts that had convinced me I needed them to survive.

When you're living a fast life, you don't easily recognize how far you've spiraled until you slam into reality. You're simply trying to enjoy yourself while being influenced by other people around you, who don't mean you any better than you mean yourself. Shoot, most of those folk have the same problems you have. That's exactly what happened with me and the gangs. The gangs caused turmoil within themselves, but then we compounded the problem by trying to delve into relationships with girls. With my alcohol, drugs, my girls, and my gang, I felt good and got puffed up. I started seeing myself as a gang leader. The thing was, my friends saw themselves as gang leaders, too. You know where that's leading to…

One of my good friends (I won't call his name out in this book) was indoctrinated so deep in the Black Panthers' culture he started passing down books and paraphernalia until we were indoctrinated, too. I assumed the Black Panther mentality and the hate that came with it. I hated people for my problems, which I believed were systematic racism. The more I indulged in the culture, the more anger consumed me. I started rebelling against racism and the people I believed were responsible for fueling it. The way I saw it, their prejudice was punishing us for who we were and hindering us from who we could be. Now I didn't steal, but I acted out in other ways: fighting, randomly busting windows out of buildings, and getting into mischievous things that I assumed would be a solution. The funny thing was that my self-inflicted *problem fixers* only made things worse.

I want you to remember that through all of this, my grandmother was still extremely active in our lives, still trying to get us delivered with those Pentecostal teachings. She was trying to get my siblings and me into church, but I didn't want to hear anything about church. I was growing up to be a man, but I wasn't there yet. See, I didn't have the knowledge nor the ability to understand what it meant to be a man in the first place. Outside of that, the enemy had me on a roll, shaping and influencing me to do wrong. Little did I know, the ram I'd always heard about growing up was already waiting in the bush to rescue me.

Around this time, my oldest sister, Joyce, had moved to Dallas, gotten saved, and converted into the Full Gospel church. Joyce was the only one of us who was in church and talked to us about the Lord, even though I personally wasn't trying to hear it. God was the furthest thing from my mind! "You need to get your life together," Joyce told me. "You're young, you have a full life ahead of you, and you need to slow down!"

In my eyes, I wasn't going fast enough.

I loved my sister, but who was she to try to put the brakes on everything I planned to do? I had a lot to offer. I was hanging out with people who were a lot older than me and maturing at a fast rate. That's where I fit in and where I wanted to stay. By then, we were immersed so deep in the Black Panthers' movement there was no turning back. In fact, my friend contacted a group of Panthers out of Oakland, CA, and invited them to come to Texas to meet us. Things were so bad when they came down; we were on the verge of a race war. Local police had converged on the town and recruited the help of officers from other areas as well. All because the three Black Panthers they heard were coming to town. It was shaping up to be a race riot. I welcomed that. I craved it. An outbreak would allow me to flex my muscles and prove I wasn't to be messed with. That would show my sister and everyone who doubted me, who was in charge, and who would come out on top. I thought I was hot, somebody. And no one could tell me different.

So, the Panthers came down, talked, and shared some things with us. To put things in perspective, my friends and I were younger, so they told us we could become junior Panthers and full-fledged members once we were older. I already thought I was somebody, but they gave me the status quo to get even more puffed up.

Man, things got worse. I sank lower and lower, growing further away from God than I truly intended. God knows I needed to be closer to Him more than ever, no matter how hard I ran away from Him. Going down the wrong trail, I grew worse and worse. I'll never forget having a conversation with my sister one day before she went back to Dallas. "You need to get in church," she admonished me. "I think if you change your life, the rest of them (my circle and brothers) will as well." Being the middle child, this didn't make much sense to me. *How could I have a greater influence on my older brothers than they had on me?*

I was more radical than my siblings. My sister only told me those things because she wanted me to see in myself what she and so many others saw in me. The ability to lead people was already on me; I just hadn't owned it. I was oblivious to my power to influence others to follow me, even if it was in the wrong direction.

Once, my friends and I managed to pull some money together and had some folks buy a couple of guns for us. That really made us think we were ready for anything, man. On top of that, we carried Dollar Specials (switchblades) to the other side of town, where we got into squabbles, fights, and violence. Violence was embedded in my nature. I became a child of wrath and thirsty to do devious things because I thought it made me royalty. I'll never forget a cousin of mine and another young man on the block who got involved with the same young lady. Once they got to arguing over her, the rest of us made it our business and got involved, too, all over a girl. Looking back, it was nonsense, but it was enough to put an entire city against another back then.

"You need to stay out of this," my sister warned me. "I saw something bad about you in this dream. I don't like this…I had a dream about you."

"I don't even believe in dreams," I laughed off what my sister said, as most young people do. Soon enough, that same laughter would change to tears. And I tell you, later that same night, God would once again prove just how great He is.

Somewhere between 10:30 p.m. and midnight, a group of us sat outside in a yard, assuming we had everything under control. My brother and some other young guys went to a place called Buddie's Diner to grab some food while the rest of us sat around chucking it up, laughing without a care in the world. We had no idea how death was hovering over us. What happened next has been forever engraved in my heart, never to leave.

My cousin, our friend, Homer, and I congregated, leaning on a car. Suddenly, a guy came out from under the porch, wielding a 12-gage shotgun and waving it at us. Lord, Jesus! I was fifteen years old. Fifteen!! Thinking I was about this life. Staring down the gun barrel showed me how far from that life I was.

"Is that you?" the guy growled at my cousin, using a name none of us were familiar with. When my cousin didn't answer, he turned to me. "Is it you?"

"No, that's not me! That's not me!" I answered.

Angrily, he turned to our friend, calling him by his name as the gun shook in his hands.

"Yeah, that's me," he confirmed.

Our friend stood on the porch, and my cousin and I were on the ground. Holding the gun steady, the guy narrowed his eyes. "Get over there and stand together," he ordered.

Even though I didn't have the desire to serve Him, if there was any time I needed God, I knew I needed Him right then and there. I didn't know a thing about guns, but I knew how to pray.

God, have mercy on me! Please spare my life! I prayed like I had never prayed before.

While praying, I heard my cousin and the other guy apologizing, saying it wasn't them the gunman was looking for. "I'm gonna kill you," the gunman roared, "Shut up!"

The gunman was so close I felt his breath brushing against my face. No more than three feet away from the gun barrel, I squeezed my eyes shut, praying harder.

Lord, if You'll just spare my life!

Boom!

My eyes shot open.

All I saw were flashes of blue and red. My vision was completely blurred, and I was too stunned to focus beyond all the different colors I saw. A weight that felt like a gooey mass fell on top of my hands, bringing everything into focus. The gun was pointed in my direction; the shooter began backing up.

"Let's go!" my friend screamed. But I couldn't move. I held my hands in front of me, but not in a posture of worship. My entire body quaked. In my hands were my cousin's intestines, blown out by an assailant known to us all. I wanted to vomit, but the horror I felt wouldn't spew out. Blood was all over my hands and my clothes. I wasn't a man. I was a kid. A kid hovering over his cousin's body as he wailed in misery.

Scream. Cry. Curse. Run.

I didn't know what to do.

Witnessing my cousin being shot put terror in me. I laid him on the ground while my friend stood on the porch in a state of shock, screaming and running in circles. "Shut up," I hollered at him. "We need to get some help!" It was all I could do to calm him down while trying to comfort my cousin at the same time. His moans haunted me. All I wanted to do was take the pain away.

The blood. There was so much blood. After an eternity, help finally came.

I'll never forget my aunt's cries over her son. "Son, son!" she cried. "Can you hear me?"

"Mama, mama!" he gurgled in response.

The medics took my cousin away as police converged on the scene and took me downtown. At the station, one of the detectives informed me the assailant had been apprehended. After identifying him as the shooter, I was shown a gory picture of my cousin lying on the stretcher, consumed by his insides and blood. My cousin was pronounced dead upon arrival; I was devastated.

That night and a slew of others to follow left me unable to sleep. Behind my closed lids, the continuous vision of my slaughtered cousin haunted me. I tossed, turned, and tried to keep from throwing up, staring into the darkness, and searching for the light.

"You spared my life. You had mercy on me," I informed God as if He wasn't aware. "If it had not been for You..." my voice trailed off in the darkness.

God had watched over me. Had He not been watching over me, I wouldn't be writing this book. Or, someone else would be writing it about me. Most likely, if God hadn't intervened, I'd have been lifting my eyes from hell.

"You need to get out of Longview," my sister and so many others told me later on. "It's dangerous, and you're already in enough trouble. You need to go."

Another of my sisters offered to stay with her in Dallas. As a 17-year-old in 1969 with no other options, I took her up on it.

Enough time had passed, and I was on a different course. Relocating to a huge city I wasn't familiar with left me facing how to deal with life all over again. *Do I turn to my old ways, back to everything I already knew? Or do I finally learn how to change?*

CHAPTER Three

Military Man

"The steps of a good man are ordered by the Lord: and he delighteth in his way."

~ Psalm 37:23, KJV

Life has a way of showing us our path, especially those things we least expect.

Dallas was so different. Scary, almost. Learning my way around a big city that felt nothing like Longview was challenging, even if it was safer for me. The one good thing about moving here was reuniting with my girlfriend...my future wife. (*Yes, I'm smiling*). Who would have known I'd leave the claws of danger to come all the way up here to find the love of my life? Now with her by my side, I had to navigate my way through this new environment. I didn't have a job, a car, or know my way around the city. My sister,

Karlene, was trying her best to teach me the ropes around Dallas, which was good for me since my girl stayed in South Dallas, and I was in Oak Cliff. If this thing would work, I would have a lot of learning to do.

Eventually, life began looking up. I secured a job that taught me discipline, responsibility, and more about life. Without my parents and brothers to lean on, I had to learn to stand on my own and be a man all by myself. It's funny how God will put you in a place of isolation to prove He exists and how much we need Him in our lives. It was tight, but slowly, I began to feel more comfortable. My sister, Joyce, took me to the Full Gospel Church with her, yet I still wasn't ready to convert to Christianity. The thirst for that rowdy nature, that radical spirit in me, dominated my desires. My location changed, but the mentality remained the same. I refused to be held accountable for my failures, still blaming others for my stumbles. Life had been bitter to me, and it wasn't my fault. At least, that's not the way I saw it.

I was working, burning the midnight oil, and driving a bit. Teresa and I were hanging out, going to the movies, the zoo, and enjoying each other's company. To my surprise, Homer (the friend who was with me the fateful night my cousin was murdered) moved to Dallas to escape trouble, just as I had. He and I reconnected, picking up where we'd left off and bonding over the tragedy that sealed us as brothers. Having him around to talk to was a relief. We helped each other get our feelings out and finally put it all behind us. Things felt like they were changing, but I was still running down the wrong track.

With a little money in my pocket and moving up in life, my drinking increased. There was a time when I didn't drink wine, but I even started drinking that. True to my old self, my circle had grown with a number of friends who were criminals. I thought they were teaching me how to cope; in actuality, I was being dragged down even lower than I'd ever been. Sometimes we think we're ahead and have everything together, but there'll always be something that creeps up to set us back. But God has a plan for our lives, even when we can't see it.

Teresa and I started talking about marriage. We had so many things we wanted to accomplish that we outlined our goals for the next two years together. Even though I was staying with my sister, I could support myself, which made dreaming with Teresa easier. Our goals seemed attainable, and I was hungry for them. The thing is, I was supporting my habits, too. Didn't even think twice about it because I was on "Cloud 9." Things were looking good. Fantastic, even. My future looked great...but not for long.

One day, my sister called and told me that one of my brothers in Longview called to say a letter from the U.S. Government had arrived at the East Texas house for me. Selective Service. My brother offered to open the letter and read it to me, but in the pit of my stomach, I already knew what to expect, so I told him I'd come to pick it up and read it for myself.

Longview is only a little over two hours outside of Dallas, so I made plans to go down and see what this piece of mail was all about. A couple of days later, I was holding the letter that would shift my life yet once again:

Greetings from the President of the United States of America, You have been hereby drafted into the US Army and are hereby ordered out with your draft to go into the Vietnam War.

My heart sank.

Same rollercoaster, spiraling down once again.

Drafted? Me? Into the army?

I didn't know a thing about armies except the gangs I'd been in. My knowledge failed to extend beyond the stories I'd heard about soldiers being returned home in body bags. This war had snatched so many people's loved ones away, leaving destruction and devastation in its wake. The tales of young boys my age traveling to the other side of the world to fight a war they had nothing to do with or knew anything about chilled my bones like they were covered in massive bricks of ice. Now, my name was included on that roster? I had to fight a battle I hadn't started.

No! This couldn't be my fate. Not me! Why did I have to be part of this war?

I felt angry and betrayed like the system was dragging me back down when I'd just come up. I escaped to Dallas to be in a safe environment where I could live in peace and survive. Things were going well, and my life had become brand new. But the letter I crinkled in my hands told me I had 30 days before this whole new world – and possibly my life, would be taken from me.

30 days!!

That time frame stayed on me like a nightmare I couldn't wake up from. Thirty days to take the physical required for army enrollment. Thirty days to inform my job and make preparations for my departure. Thirty days before I'd have to leave my sweet Teresa behind. Thirty days to wonder what was going to happen to me.

I was put on a bus to Shreveport, where I was among hundreds of young men lined up to take our physicals. It was a whirlwind of doctors, each scrambling to get us in and out as quickly as possible, like an assembly line. This one checked our eyes, that one looked up our nose, another checked the other body parts the previous doctors hadn't gotten to. Then we had to get dressed and were ushered by men in uniforms who conducted a quick, informal ceremony. "You are now inducted into the United States Army," their stoic voices boomed.

I lifted my hand and took the oath before a piece of paper was shoved in my hand.

"In 30 days, you will be gone to Vietnam – Saigon," one of the officers said.

If it's possible to hear something heartbreaking, mine shrieked across the crowded room. The disappointment burst so loud in my ears; I thought my hearing was lost. There wasn't a sound other than my heart slowly beating to the count of the time left on the calendar before I had to surrender my freedom to the government.

"In three days, you'll be taken to Fort Dix for training," the officer's melancholy voice snapped me back to attention. Everything after that is a blur, except for the bus ride back to downtown Longview, where I was dropped off. Always the schemer, my mind was already swirling with various ways I could escape this mess. *Some kind of way, I'm going to get out of this*, I thought.

I hopped off the bus and raced to the Air Force recruiter's office for help. The gentleman inside the office informed me that they had closed at 5:30 p.m., but they could take me to Tyler and get tested for enlistment in the Air Force as long as I passed. I didn't care what the details were; I just wanted to avoid going to Vietnam. Not only did I take the Air Force test, I passed it and was immediately sworn in. Placed on a 30-day delay, I returned home to my sister and Teresa, telling them what had happened. Life in the military was about to begin. I may not have known what was coming next, but at least I was safe from the war.

CHAPTER Four

War Zone

"Put on the full armor of God, so that you can take your stand against the devil's schemes"

~ Ephesians 6:11, NIV

So, after being drafted into the U.S. Army, I volunteered for the Air Force and completed basic training.

#53.

I'll never forget the sound of my draft lottery number exploding in my ears as I read it, like the sound of fireworks being set off during an Independence Day celebration. Only, I was losing my own. The paperwork I received indicated that I would be deployed to Vietnam immediately following basic training. My workaround to get out of traveling there was volunteering for a four-year stint instead of two. After all I had done to scheme and secure my comfort, safety, and peace of mind, I still wound up going to Southeast Asia, impacting my life more than the nightmares I initially imagined going there to be.

Coming from a small city and being thrust into an intense environment with people from all over the world was jarring for my mental health and my soul. The military is where I learned the true power of the influence other people can have on us. My life went from petty squabbles on the streets to total despair. At the time, I was only 19. I'd dabbled in marijuana, but nothing major. However, in my desire to fit in with my roommate and friends I'd made in the barracks, I succumbed to the equivalent of peer pressure, sacrificing myself for a hit of drugs and a dose of misconstrued notoriety.

Now marijuana on its own was one thing, but I began experimenting with opium-laced marijuana, which was an entirely different danger. The soldiers would take a string, dip them in opium, then lace the string around the joints. They called the sticks "Mr. Buddha," and "Mr. Buddha" quickly got us addicted to him. For a bit of reference, Buddha is a religious symbol in Asian culture, with an overwhelming presence. In deciding to try the drug bearing the mere name Buddha, I failed to realize that I was attaching myself to the addiction that came with it.

I was stationed overseas for 15 months. I began smoking a little, but eventually, my body was unintentionally transformed from my former fit self to a man I barely recognized. No matter how much my physical form was altered, I desired more and more. The opium had such a stronghold on me I no longer craved the high I got when it was paired with lesser drugs; I needed it strong and outright. I even put it in Smack – cigarettes that replaced tobacco with opium.

The "payoffs" from my highs weren't as invigorating as I thought they would be, not in the flesh. My entire life was altered by something bigger than me that I couldn't control. God moved further and further away from my mind; all I could think about was doing wrong. But even though I was at my worst, God still held me close to His heart. I have no doubt about that.

Now there were two young men (one from Baltimore and the other from Washington) who observed me from the sidelines. They began witnessing to me and encouraging me to attend church on the base. Remarkably, I promised to attend a service and actually showed up. While there, I listened to the message; however, I didn't receive it. As soon as the benediction hit and I was on the other side of the church's front door, I was back at it again. One good thing did come from my church excursion, though. Being in a foreign land, away from all the people I'd grown up with and known my entire life, forced me to pray.

At this point, drugs ruled my life. Addiction was attached to my every move. It wasn't just that I was doing drugs just to do them – that war had such a horrific effect on the soldiers that our emotional destruction without using drugs was inevitable. Many soldiers cracked under the pressure of wanting to go home. Others who were married received "Dear John" letters from their spouses, announcing they were seeking a divorce so they could move on with their lives instead of waiting for their love to return home.

One incident ingrained in my memory from that war

changed me more than any drug I consumed could ever come close to doing. This war was about fighting an "enemy," but the effects turned us against ourselves. No longer did we think the same, move the same, or even walk the same as we were constantly enshrouded in fear. One of the darkest moments of my life was standing before an MP (military police), who took out a gun, put it to his head, and blew his brains out right in front of me. He couldn't bear the pressure any longer, and he wasn't the only one.

We went downtown to get our drugs. With all the turmoil surrounding me, I began taking more and more pills to numb myself to the new reality I was living in. Every now and then, I would call my family back home. One day, I called to speak with my sister – a true warrior for God.

"How are you?" she asked with as much care as she could muster, given the circumstances.

"I'm fine," I lied.

We went on to chat a bit longer, but when it grew to be too heavy for me, I disconnected the call.

Later that evening, I went downtown to party with a group of friends. I swallowed 14 "downers," chased with alcohol and a hit of Smack. In a drug-induced stupor, I fell off the stool I'd been sitting on. Everything went black. I woke up in a friend's apartment, spanked by my friends, who were staring at me.

"We thought we lost you," one of them said. "We didn't know what to do, Ro...we just knew you were dead!"

According to them, I wasn't breathing, nor did I have a heartbeat. Panicked, they briefly considered dumping my body because had they taken me to the base, there would've been an investigation. Now that I had woken up, everyone would be safe. This wasn't a nap I'd woken up from – I was out for three days! I overdosed on a Friday night; it was Monday before I regained consciousness.

I should've been on the base, at work, and so should they. I was AWOL because I overdosed, and no one knew what to do. Now, I am more afraid than ever. My addiction was out of control, and I knew it. I called my sister and told her what happened.

"When did this happen?" she asked.

"Friday night," I reported.

My sister heaved a heavy sigh. "We were at church Friday night, praying. And when I went home, the Lord woke me up." She paused briefly to let me take in what she was about to say. "God told me to pray for you because you were on your way out, Roscoe."

I listened in stunned silence.

"I got up and prayed for you," she continued. "And I prayed, and prayed, all night long. When did you wake up?"

"Monday," I whispered.

"That's when the Lord told me He was going to restore you!"

Thank you, Jesus!

When you're doing wrong, know that God will put you on someone else's mind to intercede for you because He has you on His mind.

When I arrived in Asia, I was 150 pounds; I returned home at 85 pounds. 85 pounds!

Please hear me – I was skin and bones. This cruel addiction had almost completely eaten my flesh away. I was even on meth at the time, driven by addiction. A junkie. There's no other way to put it; that's what I was. It didn't matter that I wasn't injecting drugs into my arms with needles; I took the same stuff other junkies shot up with and either smoked it or snorted it up my nose. Now, I was going totally down.

Not only was I in a war in the trenches, I was in a spiritual war. And my mind paid the price for it.

CHAPTER Five

End Of An Era

"For I know the plans I have for you, declares the Lord, plans for welfare and not for evil, to give you a future and a hope."

~ Jeremiah 29:11, ESV

Military life sent me into a tailspin. Taiwan's culture, language, and customs were a far cry from Longview, and it took some time for me to adjust. Being stationed in a foreign country without anyone you love being around to ensure everything would be alright was grueling; however, I endured it until it was time for me to return home. Oh, I was excited to go back home!

Some of the friends I made in Taiwan joined together and decided to go to the Air Force base in Virginia. At this time, I only had two years left in the military, but my life was still in disarray. Can you imagine? Even with all the training, the drills, the discipline, the rules, and the regulations, the old me was clawing to come back out for a reappearance. Consequently, I landed on the east coast, running with the same friends I'd been running with before. We did tours together, one of which was three times to Germany, where I was introduced to "hash" – another drug.

A group of us went down to the parks in Frankfurt, bought our stash of drugs, and returned to the barracks to smoke it. From there, addiction took control of my body. Before I knew it, I'd infiltrated my body with more drugs than ever before. I took them in tandem, hoping the different effects would cater to the high I craved; however, there was so much that I felt the chase of the high more than the actual effects of the drugs. I'd done drugs across Europe and Southeast Asia; adding hash into the mix only intensified my need for something greater. Nothing satisfied me, and my body began rejecting the "minor" drugs. I was desperate for something stronger.

Methamphetamines. Acid. Speed. LSD. These were all the drugs in my arsenal that drove me further and further away from God. I was in my own world, a bubble of addiction that wouldn't break. It's hard to explain, but these hallucinating drugs made it hard to differentiate reality from imagination. They even led to hearing voices that weren't there. When I was on my acid trips, the voices would scream, pouncing like demons trying to talk to me. The funny thing is, even though I wasn't trying to get close to God, I called out to Him to bring me down from my high. I begged Him for relief. I cried out, knowing He was my only help in slaying the demons that had overtaken me. Sometimes the high lasted two or three days. "Lord, help get me off these drugs!" I hollered out. But as soon as the high went down, I went right back for more.

I returned to Virginia from training, just like the song says, "*Runaway child, running wild. You better get back home...*"

I was running from God, myself, and the pain of feeling alone. My time in the military was winding down, and I was staying closer to home. Out of all the uncertainty I was going through, one thing was for sure – once my time was up, I was out of the military.

I told Teresa I was getting out of the service and that we were going to get our lives together – together as one. Several years passed, and it was the summer of 1976. I'd been on the east coast for a little over two years and was transferred to Dallas Air Force Base in Abilene. By the grace of God, I received an honorable discharge and returned home to Teresa, who was waiting for me with open arms.

Teresa had an apartment and was pretty much set with everything we needed. I didn't open up initially, but she noticed how much weight I'd lost since she'd last seen me. I was a lot bonier than I used to be. (I can laugh about that now.) She had proven to be a rock and source of comfort for me. She didn't make me feel judged or disrespected. I trusted Teresa wholeheartedly and knew I wanted to spend the rest of my life with her. She graciously listened as I unraveled what I'd been through, the horrors I'd experienced, and the trauma I had yet to recover from. But she was there. And that was all I needed.

September 20, 1976, I married the love of my life. I was still an addict, but Teresa accepted me as I was. The worst part of her allegiance to me was trapping her and my siblings in the throes of my addiction. That's right – my wife, my brothers, and my sisters were all addicted to marijuana and pills because I introduced them to them. I was a leader in getting people to do wrong. Including my own blood and the woman I vowed to cherish and protect forever. The devil used me to force all of them down the road to destruction I was traveling. As the scripture says, if the blind lead the blind, then we'll all fall into a ditch. Every one of us was blinded.

To put it in perspective, I was a 23-year-old married man who didn't feel the responsibility of matrimony. The only thing I'd known all my life was the military and drugs. Don't get me wrong – Teresa and I enjoyed life, but it wasn't the life God intended for us. We were wasting money, constantly partying, hanging out at concerts, and such. The Air Force trained me but had failed to erase the bad habits asphyxiating my soul. I can say right here that God never gave up on me. He is still God in my life! He never gives up on us, even when we give up on Him.

Friendships hit differently when you're tripping on drugs together. Are you truly friends, or does a common demon bind you while everybody's getting high?

I was on Overton Road in Oak Cliff, talking with my friends about who we were and what we did when one of the guys with us decided to challenge me about what he could do and I couldn't do. Well, this led to a nasty dispute. As we argued back and forth, I grew more aggressive, and so did he.

"Do you know who I am?" he seethed.

Now why would he ask a man who was ungodly and full of vanity that question? I enjoyed cursing folks out, and loved to fight, so answering him wasn't but a thing for me. "I don't care who you are," I shot back. I'm high, tripping, barely able to see, and ready to finish what the brother was trying to start with me. In my fog, I clearly saw the guy pull out a nickel-plated .38 pistol and put it to my head.

"Uh-huh, negro," he hissed, "let me show you something."

He pulled the trigger.

Click, click, click!

...nothing. The chain had broken!

Stunned, I backed away. My would-be killer was just as stunned as I was. Maybe more.

"Who are you?" His voice rang in the silence, waving the gun in the air. "I pulled this trigger six times, and nothing went off. Who are you?" he demanded again. I gulped as I watched him open the gun and empty the bullets intended for me into the palm of his opposite hand as proof of the miracle.

One, two, three, four, five, six.

My entire body quaked. The chamber had been full, but I was still alive.

God, I should've been dead, I thought. Not one single bullet had pierced my temple. God had truly covered me. He spared my life... again. Out of all the things I'd done, the drugs, the fights, the reckless nights, and endless days of trying to prove a worth I myself didn't need. The devil had me again, but God, in His goodness, had spared my life *again!*

That word rings in my spirit: AGAIN!

Now one would think that at this point, I would've gotten up and beat the pastor to church. Sadly, I didn't. My attitude was that my cunning ways had gotten me out of another bind. By my standards, I saved myself, and I was invincible. It sounds ridiculous now, but that's the world that addiction creates. It's dark, one-sided, evil, and manipulative. When you're driven by the devil, you believe life can't take you out. That's exactly what swirled through my mind as I got haughty with arrogance at surviving karma yet again.

At some point, I realized I needed a change, but I still wrestled with breaking up with my old ways. I continued running wild, married but single, partying, and doing anything I wanted. My wife at home didn't matter. I was married to "that life." Don't get me wrong, I felt like marrying Teresa was the best thing that happened to me because I loved her. And I still do. But the streets kept calling, refusing to break the hold they had on me. I was out there having such a good time; I didn't even realize how close I was to losing my "good thing" until we separated because of my ways.

A year passed after I'd married Teresa. She had something to tell me but was too nervous, so she told my sister to drop the news on me instead.

"Teresa thinks she's pregnant," my sister said.

Oh my God.

I wasn't ready.

The carton of milk I was holding hit the floor with a thud. I was elated, but my excitement was short-lived when the painful reminder that I wasn't together with my wife slammed me. I already messed things up so badly that we were living apart. We allowed our problems to get in the way of us. We'd come through too much to throw it all away, especially now that another life – a blessing, had suddenly changed our family dynamic. Not only were we going through the madness together, but Teresa had also faced some horrible situations herself, which I'm sure she'll share later when she's ready.

A baby was coming to count on me, a future father who was still outrunning bullets, the police, time, and destiny. I even had a guy threaten to kill me with a razor. My life was a mess. I was an unhappy, disturbed young man on the run from God. But I darted from the Father straight into trouble because trouble was where I felt safe.

My first child, Andre, roared into this world, stealing my heart. Two years later, we had another child, my daughter, Shaneri. By our third child, Kermitrice, Teresa and I were still running crazy instead of settling down like we were parents. We were moving in and out of apartments, racking up evictions while I still entertained drugs to numb the world around me. I loved my family, but the responsibility for their well-being was overwhelming. Drugs were dragging my life down, but I just couldn't seem to kick them. Consequently, I couldn't hold a job for long, and paycheck-to-paycheck stretched too far in between.

When you're constantly high, you're unable to produce. Not even my own family could help me shake it. My instability caused us to go from pillar to post, migrating from place to place like nomads. When Teresa discovered she was pregnant with our third child, she came to me and told me she didn't want to have another baby.

"I want an abortion." The weariness in her voice shook me. She was tired, but I was adamant.

"No!" I told her. "I don't believe in abortion, and I don't want to hear nothing about you having one. No, we're not doing it."

"I don't care what you say. This is what we're going to do." Teresa's tone grew firm, her body language stiff and unmovable.

"I said no!" I walked away before our discussion turned into something bigger. Had we been the best parents? No one would give us any awards for how we dragged our children from spot to spot, resting our heads until the next eviction notice came. But there was no way I was going to let Teresa take our child away from us. The child deserved to live, even if our conditions weren't completely livable.

We were disappointed. Finances were in disarray. Neither of us had a reliable income, and what little money we had went straight out the door to support my drug habit instead of my wife and children. I made sure there was enough money to keep my stash before I paid the bills, even though the drugs had ravished my body. I told Teresa we needed to keep our child, but I was only concerned about the next high. In fact, Teresa worked herself to the bone to keep our family afloat while I used my time to wallow in my mess. Any money I made went right back to the drug dealers I bought from. It was a vicious cycle that couldn't be broken.

As things around me disintegrated further, all I could think was, *where do I go from here?*

I didn't want God. I didn't want the devil either, but that joker had a grip on me. No one could tell me anything because I already knew everything. My attitude was *leave me alone and let me enjoy my high*. It was good while it lasted. See, every good thing in life must come to an end, even when we are enjoying them. We eventually come to a point where we have to make a choice.

And I had a huge one to make.

CHAPTER Six

He Came To See About Me

*"The Lord is near to all who call on him,
to all who call on him in truth."*

~ Psalm 145:18, NIV

One would think that after having children, things would have gotten better for me and that I would have desired more for myself and my family. I absolutely loved them with every part of me, but the drugs had too strong of a hold on me. My kids should have provoked me into becoming the man I *should've* been, but the devil had more power over me than they did.

My life had become a black hole with no signs of light. My heart was beating, but I wasn't breathing. My feet walked, but I was unable to move. This is what I'd become: a drug addict consumed by a love of all the wrong things life offered me. I'd reached the point of no return. But that's when miracles do their best work, right?

So, there I was, floating along, wasting away in my own guilt and failures. In a totally unexpected move, I had an encounter with God, which left me shaken. It started strangely, but we never know how God will deal with us, myself included.

My brother Herbert and I were close, bonded by our vices. Herbert was an alcoholic, so we dealt with many of the same circumstances. I traveled to visit him on the weekends, grateful to have someone to hang with and talk to. My sister used to witness to both of us about Christ, but just like me, Herbert wasn't trying to hear it. I wasn't the only one running away, fighting against God. But one day, Herbert confided to me that another of our brothers had taken him to a Pentecostal church, and his heart had been pricked. Herbert was about to get baptized.

The strangest thing happened on the day of the baptism. As he stood outside the water, prepared to step in, Herbert had a change of heart. He didn't want to be saved. "Roscoe, I almost made a change," he called to report. "I almost got saved."

"What happened?" I wanted to know.

Herbert took a deep breath before recounting what happened. "They got me there, and I almost got baptized. I got ready to put my feet in the water, but I changed my mind."

My natural instinct should have been to encourage my brother, but remember – I thought I didn't need Jesus in my life. "That's good; I'm glad you didn't!" I said indignantly. "You don't need Jesus; they were trying to get you!"

All this time, I assumed *they* were out to get us. *They*, being church folks. That's what the devil was swaying me to believe. In reality, the people who loved and cared about me were only trying to *get us* to come to Christ, so our lives would be better. Herbert and I laughed about that like we were at a comedy show.

"I'll see you in about another week or so," I told Herbert before our conversation ended.

A week later, my sister called and told me to get back down there because Herbert had fallen extremely ill. I hit the road and stopped at my mother's house, where my brother stayed. As usual, I knocked on the door when I arrived, but there was no response.

"Herbert," I shouted, "get up and open the door!"

A bit of scrambling alerted me that someone was inside, so I knocked again until the door swung open.

"What's up, Herbert? Why are you sitting in the dark?" I stepped inside, scanning the house. "Why is it so dark in here?" I wandered further inside as Herbert closed and secured the door.

"I was trying to find Jesus," Herbert murmured.

I was incredulous. "Trying to find Jesus? I don't understand?"

"I was trying to find Jesus," Herbert repeated. "And I haven't been able to."

I glared at Herbert as if he'd lost his mind. "What is wrong with you?" Herbert held his side, wincing in pain. "I'm taking you to the doctor to find out what's wrong with you."

I gathered Herbert and my mother and raced to the hospital. After examining my brother, the doctor came to me, holding an X-ray. "I need you to look at this," he said.

I peered at the film, unsure what I was looking at.

"You see this?" the doctor pointed at a spot on the picture. "This is Herbert's lung. You see this black part, the size of a fist?"

I nodded. "Yes, but what are you saying, doctor?"

"Herbert's lungs are being eaten up," the doctor confirmed. "Your brother's lungs are literally being eaten up. They've deteriorated so badly; there's hardly any lung left."

My heart shot down to the pit of my stomach. I forced myself not to panic, but on the inside, I was screaming. I knew what was happening but needed to hear it directly from my brother's caretaker. "What are you saying, doctor?"

"Your brother will not live another day," the doctor blurted. "Within 24 hours, he will be dead."

Listening to the doctor in disbelief, a harsh chill froze me down to my veins.

"I know," Herbert said soberly. "I know I'm dying. That's why I was trying to find Jesus."

My mother and I began weeping; however, Herbert was resigned to his grave fate. We took him back home and delivered the grim diagnosis to my sister, who took him to the VA hospital in Shreveport, Louisiana, in a desperate attempt to save his life while I jumped in my car and headed back home.

When I arrived in Dallas, Teresa told me to call my sister.

"When I got Herbert here, he fell out of the wheelchair and died," she sobbed over the phone.

An unexplainable wave of mourning, grief, and terror gripped my soul. I was devastated! My brother, my friend, and my confidant was gone. I hadn't experienced pain like this before. None of us had. Herbert was our first sibling to die. I was completely shattered. My closest ally in the world had been savagely snatched from me. What more did God want from me?!?!

Once the arrangements had been made, I went back to Longview for the wake for the viewing. I felt hollow inside as everyone passed the casket, weeping over my brother. Soon enough, it was my turn to say goodbye. I crept to the coffin like an apprehensive sinner approaching the altar. I stood there before my late brother, and I cried and cried. To this day, I don't understand why I cried so much. That wasn't me. I wasn't an emotional person like that.

I thought the tears had dried up, and I strolled away from the casket. But I found myself up there again, crying harder than before.

"Why are you crying so much, Roscoe?" my paternal grandmother asked. "Herbert is gone now; everybody's doing alright."

My teary eyes burned as I lifted them to stare into hers. "You don't understand how I'm hurting."

Everyone at the wake had straightened up as though they weren't sobbing minutes before. Not me. I couldn't shake the devastation from my spirit. There was no way Herbert deserved just a mere few minutes of honor in his memory. Why wasn't everyone torn up like I was? I wept like I'd lost the best thing in my life.

I wept because it could've been me.

Later on, I told my sister Karlene. "Let's go to Dreamland Inn so that we can put this behind us."

Karlene agreed, but two of my other sisters who'd gotten saved had other plans. They interrupted me as I was getting dressed, suggesting I go to church with them rather than the club.

"Don't talk to me about no church," I snapped. "I'm going out to party, have a good time, and put all this behind me."

"We're going to pray for you," my sisters said.

I laughed in their faces. "Pray all you want to. You can pray all night long. Ain't nothing gonna bind me," I said before ushering them out the door and closing it behind them.

Sitting in the den alone, I laughed. *I told them something,* I thought.

I reached into my sock and pulled out my stash – weed, preludes, quaaludes, uppers, and downers. Everything I needed to take the pain away was stuffed in there. I released a twisted laugh as I sat rolling a joint, thinking about how I'd told my sisters off. Their prayers sailed through the walls, making me chuckle even harder.

In the midst of my ignoring their prayers, something strange happened. Out of nowhere, a voice called out, *Put those drugs down!*

My head jerked, and I looked around the room. Of course, I didn't see anyone because I was alone there, but I still knew I heard something.

Put those drugs down, get up, and go to church! The voice grew sterner as it chastised me. *Because where your brother lies, so shall ye lie also.*

Without having to see Him, I knew it was the voice of God I was hearing.

I jumped up, scrambled across the room, and slung the door open. My sisters were still out there praying, and I raced past them, straight to the phone to call my brother Matthew. "Take me to church," I pleaded. "I feel like my life is over. I've got to go to church!"

"What do you mean? You don't go to church," Matthew said.

"Yeah, I know, but God is telling me if I don't go to church, I'm going to be where Herbert's at!" The words caught in my throat, but I managed to get them out to plead my case.

A short time later, I was in church, shaking and trembling with the fear of God. Those who knew me looked upon me in confusion. The Roscoe they saw sitting in the pews wasn't the same man they had come to know. Outward fear wasn't me. They knew that. But the encounter with God had literally shaken me so much that I felt like I had to get to the Father, or my life was over. Weeping over Herbert made sense now. I was weeping for myself.

It was Saturday night, and Easter was the next morning. I cried all night long in church as the saints prayed over me. "I'm going to church tomorrow," I told Teresa and my siblings.

"Aren't you the one who told us not to go to church?" came their collective sentiment. "You told Herbert not to get baptized!"

The truth was in my face. "Yes, I did. But you don't understand; I heard a voice speak to me, and I must go."

They said I was out of my mind and hearing things. But I knew without a doubt what I'd heard. Even Teresa told me not to go because I was fine where I was at.

Despite what anyone said, I pressed my way to church on Easter Sunday morning. My siblings tagged along, really, to see what I was going to do. Now I admit that I played about going to church in the past. I pretended to be on my way; then, I'd stop at the liquor store to grab some drinks. My excuse? I could party and praise God at the same time. The difference between then and now was that God really had touched my heart this time. This time was for real.

The preacher delivering the Word that day (I'll call him "Jones") was a great man of God and a wonderful speaker. The topic that day was, *Whose fool are you?* Are you a fool for God or one for the devil? I know people have said this before, but as Jones preached, I thought he was preaching directly to me. His words shot straight into my heart.

"You fool," rang in my ears, over and over again.

Tears streamed from my eyes and soaked my face. It was a complete contradiction to the cruel, mean, cursing blasphemer I'd been all this time. I didn't care. As soon as the preacher asked who wanted to be saved, I darted from my chair and dashed to the altar without looking back. I ran up there so fast; I didn't even notice my sister running beside me. She stood with me at the altar, both of us crying out as the church looked on. My grandmother and the congregation stared at me in disbelief; I barely believed what was happening myself. But there was no turning back. I was about to be baptized.

Standing at the baptism pool was surreal. I was in the same position I'd encouraged Herbert to denounce. The people were jumping, shouting, and watching me with pride in their eyes. I lifted my hand and waved. I wasn't telling the people goodbye; I was saying goodbye to the world. After that encounter with God, I would never be the same. He made sure I was confident in that.

It was a blur, but I was baptized and tarried for the Holy Ghost. My eyes were closed, but I saw a red ball of fire behind my closed lids. I was being renewed. Later, the pastor gave me a card and asked where I lived. I told him I lived in Dallas, and he told me to reach out to his friend, Clifford Frazier, who was launching a church here.

"Pastor Frazier would be more than happy to have you there," he told me.

I took the card and went back home, a completely changed man. There was a strong tug for me to do good. Even something as simple as seeing a man on the street who may have needed a ride made me want to stop and help. My entire mindset was different. I used to fight to hurt people; now, I want to fight to help them.

Now, Teresa was skeptical when I got back home and told her I'd changed. "Those people got you messed up," she said. "You let them put all that nonsense in your head."

I knew it was hard for Teresa to understand something I hardly understood myself. Instead of getting angry, I pulled out the card and contacted Pastor Frazier, who brought Deacon Johnny over with him to the house. I notified my entire family that Pastor Frazier was coming to talk to us about the Bible. He was only expecting me, but when the gentlemen arrived, at least 12 people were waiting to hear what they had to say.

I wasn't used to all that crying, but I found myself crying again. After the men ministered to us, I took an old Bible that I had never read and marked three scriptures Pastor Frazier gave us to review before he returned the following week. He also said he was going to tarry with us. I had no idea what that meant, but I was ready.

Shortly after our meeting, I had my son, Andre (who was seven at the time), and my five-year-old daughter, Shaneri, with me at home alone. (Teresa was nine months pregnant with Kermitrice). The wonder of all wonders, I picked up the Bible to read. This was the first time ever in my life that instead of using the Bible as a bargaining tool with God, I was reading the scriptures to my children. I wept as I turned to Matthew and read the story of Jesus being nailed to the Cross.

"They took my Savior to the Cross," I wailed. "They took my Savior to the Cross. Why did they do that?" I cried like a baby. The change in me had begun, and all I could think about was God. Teresa came home from work to find me clearing the house of everything I felt wasn't of God. Especially the bar because it had alcohol.

"What in the world's going on with you?" Teresa demanded.

"I just want God to be pleased with me," I explained.

"You have lost your mind," she said.

I may have at one point and time, but God helped me find it.

Monday came, and it was time for the tarrying meeting. We gathered at my sister's home and tarried hard, trying to get the Holy Ghost, though none of us actually received it. After trying for so long, we sat around, finding ways to get it. I was determined not to quit until I got it.

"I'm gonna get the Holy Ghost tomorrow!" I said.

Remember, I hadn't read the Bible since I was eight; now, I am 25. Previously, I couldn't GPS my way to Genesis in the Bible; tackling it from the beginning was going to be a challenge, but I was up for it. Not only was I reading, but something inside me said I would get filled, and I had no doubt about that. I was so sure; I reiterated my thoughts out loud.

"I'm gonna get the Holy Ghost tomorrow!" I blurted.

I'd been unemployed for more than six months, doing nothing but sitting around the house and taking care of the kids. The day after the tarry service we had at the house, I was cutting our grass. My children were outside with me. It was a beautiful day, warm, and the sun was shining. The kids were standing beside me as I cut the hedges. The faster I cut, the more it sounded like the clippers were saying, "Jesus, Jesus, Jesus!"

What in the world is going on? I thought. All of a sudden, a strong wind blew through. It howled around me, strong and mighty, but nothing was moving. Having experienced tornadoes before, I thought, *Oh God – is this a tornado?*

I grabbed the kids, dashed inside the house, and closed the door. "Get down," I shouted. "Get down! There's a tornado coming!"

The wind grew stronger and whipped around the house. Andre broke away and traced to the window. "Daddy, why are we in here when everyone else is still outside?" he asked.

"They don't know there's a tornado out there!" I returned the same glare he was giving me.

For the second time, I heard the voice that had spoken to me in the den. *Go and pick up your Bible.* I was scared, but I was going to do exactly as the voice had instructed me to do. I scrambled over to where I had the Bible and scooped it in my hands. God be my witness; as I clutched the Word in my hands, a light shone through the ceiling, shining on the Bible. It wasn't my imagination; the Bible pages flipped themselves and didn't stop until reaching what they wanted me to see.

Read, the voice commanded.

> **And when the day of Pentecost was fully come, they were all with one accord in one place. And suddenly there came a sound from heaven as of a rushing mighty wind, and it filled all the house where they were sitting. - Acts 2:1-2, KJV**

Now go ye in the back room and receive the Holy Ghost, the voice directed me.

I closed my Bible, sat my children on the couch, went into the back room, and closed the door. I got down on my knees and hollered out to God. After a while, my knees got tired, but it had only been a few minutes. I lay on the bed and flipped on my back, staring at the ceiling. Folks might think I'm crazy, but I'm telling the truth; the ceiling turned into a ball of fire! Red, blue, and white sparks flew from the walls, but the fire wasn't contained. I was stunned – terrified, actually, yet I was unable to move.

A hand emerged from the fire and brushed against my lips, but it didn't burn. I was paralyzed as the hand opened my mouth and went down my throat to my stomach, and when it pulled out, I began speaking words I didn't know! My mind wondered what I was saying while my eyes stayed glued to the fire spitting from the ceiling. I thought I was losing my mind!

I spoke in tongues a few minutes more when the sound of my kids crying outside the door drummed in my ears. I struggled to peel myself from the bed to see about them, but the bed wouldn't let me go. Suddenly, the fire burst like shattered glass.

They're alright, the voice assured me. *Get up and tell someone what I've done for you.*

Just like that, I could move again. I rose from the bed and ran to my neighbors to tell them I'd received the Holy Ghost. They didn't believe me, and when I called to share the news with Teresa, she thought I was just talking. In fact, every person I called to spread the exciting news was filled with laughter and told me I was crazy. Honestly, with the consensus that I had lost my mind,

I started thinking maybe they were right. Maybe I'd imagined the entire thing, and nothing happened at all.

Pastor Frazier called and told me to come over to one of my sister's homes, where they'd tarry and see whether I had been filled. I got nervous. I didn't want to be embarrassed if I made the entire thing up in my mind, even though I truly believed in my heart what I'd seen.

When I got to the house, my sisters were there, along with my brother and an old friend. They told me to take a seat; if I'd spoken in tongues once, I was going to speak it again. A bundle of nerves, I lifted my hands. "Hallelujah," I proclaimed. A few seconds later, I was speaking in tongues again. I heard the words coming out of my mouth, but I couldn't do anything about it.

My brother jumped up and ran, rubbing his hands together. "Roscoe got it!" he sang over and over. My sister yelled, "Oh my God, he got it!"

As everyone celebrated, white smoke came under the door. The thick smoke swirled around us as we peered on in shock. "Someone's knocking on my door," my sister said. She went to the door, speaking in tongues. My brother joined in, and before we knew it, everyone was speaking in tongues. I received the Holy Ghost all over again!

Teresa was sitting at the table during the commotion. One of the pastor's daughters approached her, asking why she wasn't there with us. "Because I don't want to be," Teresa told her.

"You ought to get filled, too," the girl suggested.

"Thank you, but no. I don't want it." Teresa turned away from her, rubbing her pregnant belly.

"Well, you can at least get baptized," the girl prodded.

"What are you talking about?" Now, she had Teresa's attention.

At eight years old, little Lyric (Pastor's daughter) grabbed a Bible and pointed out the scripture where the people had gotten baptized in the name of Jesus in Acts 2:38. Out of nowhere, Teresa said, "I believe it."

We didn't waste any time! We baptized Teresa in my sister's bathtub, and she began to rejoice. She didn't get the Holy Ghost, but she still praised God. Getting filled and my wife getting saved made me more determined to go after God, even though I didn't know how. I thirsted for Him and consumed as much of His Word as I could digest at a time.

"God, please reveal yourself to me. Show me the way," I prayed.

The next morning, I got up with a prayer of thanksgiving. In my heart, I heard the voice again.

Many are called, but few are chosen. I chose you; you didn't choose Me. I ordained and anointed you to preach the gospel, but many shall come against you, but if I be for you, I'm more than the world against you. I listened intently as the voice continued. *But thou are not ready. After you are tried by the fire, thou shall come out as pure gold.*

I fell on the floor, weeping as I'd never wept before. "Thank You, Lord," I whispered. The God I'd been running away from for 25 years touched me and opened my eyes. Now, I'd come to know who God is.

CHAPTER

Seven

Miracles, Signs, and Wonders

Jesus replied, "What is impossible with man is possible with God."

~ Luke 18:27, NIV

After my experience with Him, God told me exactly what I would have to endure along my walk with Him – the tests, trials, and tribulations. It seemed as if I was deemed to go from one turmoil to the next. All I knew was that I would have to have faith that He would bring me through.

One of the first experiences that helped boost my faith was around 1985. I was a young minister, my pastor was invited to minister in Africa, and I was appointed to take his place at the church. Teresa had gotten sick, and I took her to the hospital, where she was diagnosed with the flu. Seven days later, however, she stood in front of the fireplace at our home, trembling and freezing. She couldn't get warm and contracted a fever at the same time. Something was terribly wrong; it had to be more than the flu.

Teresa's fever was so high I took her to the emergency room at St. Paul Hospital in Dallas. When checked, her temperature registered at 104 degrees; the doctor performed a spinal tap, withdrawing blood from her spinal cord. Teresa tested positive for meningitis, far more extreme than the flu and possibly deadly. Back then, there wasn't a cure for the disease, which made it even scarier.

Teresa's temperature shot up to 106, and she was immediately admitted to isolation on the third floor. **CAUTION INFECTIOUS DISEASE**, the yellow tape read outside of her room. For the next several days, a team of specialists converged upon Teresa's room, trying every optimal way of treatment they could manage. When I was able to see her, Teresa looked like a wild woman. Realizing my own wife could not recognize me, my heart shattered into a million pieces. Her hair was all over her head, and she writhed in pain as her screams thundered through the hospital.

The doctor advised me that the nurses would administer morphine hourly to ease Teresa's pain. After three days, I was summoned to the hospital to meet with a team of urologists and specialists specializing in meningitis. I was exhausted, scared, and uncertain of what the future held for my wife and me. But what the doctor asked next rocked me to the core.

"Do you have medical insurance for your wife?" he asked.

"Yes, sir," my voice trembled.

"Do you have burial insurance?"

For a brief second, the world went dark. I was taken out of my body, staring at my wife, suffering as she sprawled across the bed in the tiny room. I gulped the anxiety lodged in my throat. "Yes, sir. Why do you ask?"

The doctor lowered his eyes, raised them, and somberly looked into mine. "Most likely, your wife is not going to recover. Her fever's so high; we can't bring it down. She probably won't survive past the next four days."

So many things raced through my mind. I began to grieve right where I was standing. All my emotions gathered in a clump of confusion and wrapped around my throat. Seeing that I was unable to speak, the doctor continued.

"If your wife does survive, she will most likely be a vegetable the rest of her life because the infection has burned her brain out."

My heart sank. "Is there anything you can do?"

He shook his head. "The only thing I can recommend is ensuring the death insurance is current because you'll probably need it within the next four to five days."

The weight of his diagnosis crashed on me like a nail being hammered. I'd been on a fast that week, and this was my third day. Going into it, I didn't know why I was fasting, but now it had become clear. My sacrifice was for Teresa. I asked my sisters to keep the kids so I could do what I'd learned to do best – call on the name of Jesus.

This was five years into my walk with Christ, and I was still very young in the ministry. Still, I knew how to pray. And I prayed a lot. All night I would pray, sometimes from midnight to 6:00

a.m., nonstop. I went to my house, disconnected the phones (remember, this was before the invention of cell phones), and prayed all night.

The room was dark as I waited for a word from the Lord. I peered out the window, then glanced at my watch. I hadn't even realized that I'd been praying for close to six hours without ceasing. Didn't eat, didn't nap. The only breaks I took were to go to the restroom; then I got right back on the wall.

I peered out the window again, and a light shone through on my face. For the fourth time, I heard God's voice. *I've been standing before you from the time you started praying. I've stood and listened to your prayer. I will answer your prayer, and this is what I want you to do.*

I raised up, so I could hear more clearly.

I want you to go to the hospital and anoint my daughter with oil. Then I want you to whisper in her ear and tell her I will heal her in Jesus' name.

"Lord, they said her fever is too high for her to be saved," I reasoned.

Do what I tell you to do.

There was no arguing with God. I knew I needed to obey if I wanted my wife to live.

I got myself together and drove to St. Paul as quickly as the car's four wheels could carry me there. Teresa's shrill screams greeted me as soon as I rounded the corner to the hall where her room was. People stared at the yellow tape blocking off her room before turning to me with pity in their eyes.

"I'm sorry you have to go through this," the charge nurse tried to comfort me. "She's only getting worse and probably won't recover."

I nodded, but not in agreement with the nurse. I was agreeing with what God said. "I want to see my wife. I need to pray for her."

The nurse shook her head. "No sir, I can't let you go in. The doctors don't want anything to disturb her. She needs her rest. Let her sleep as much as she can while she goes through these final hours of pain."

Despite the nurse's refrain, I zipped past her and went to see my wife, ignoring the woman as she said she was calling for the doctor. I understood who her boss was, but I was operating under the authority of God.

I stepped inside Teresa's room, whipped out my anointing oil, and anointed her as God had instructed me to do. Then, I leaned over and whispered, "God said He's going to heal you in Jesus' name."

As soon as I said that, it was like a jolt of electricity shot through Teresa. This was the first time she'd responded to me in four days. Despite the reaction, her temperature was still soaring, and she was screaming in pain. But I prayed.

"God, according to Your Word and what You spoke to me, I speak in Jesus' name that by Your stripes, she is healed!" I sealed the prayer just as Teresa lifted her head. I grabbed her hand. "Stand up and lift your hands," I told her. This was the first time she got out of bed or responded to anyone, least of all my voice.

She was shaky, but Teresa stood and lifted her hands. "Jesus," she squealed out in a soft whimper. "Jesus."

"There you go," I encouraged her. "Say it again!"

The door opened, and I whirled around to see the nurse's stunned face just as Teresa declared the name of Jesus again.

"What are you doing?!?!" She looked at Teresa out of the bed in horror. "You're killing your wife; you're killing her!"

"No, I am praying for her!"

"Sir, you're killing her," the nurse charged again.

"She's not supposed to be out of bed, and you're going to kill her."

"She's ill," I insisted.

The nurse brushed past me, shoes clanking against the floor as she stomped over to Teresa. "She's dying!" She grabbed a thermometer and jammed it in Teresa's mouth. "Let me show you." When the time passed, she took the thermometer and raised it. The picture of her face, eyes bucked as she checked the number, is forever etched in my mind.

"What is it?" I asked.

"Oh my God..." her voice was laced with shock. "I know I just checked her an hour ago, and her fever clocked at 106." She drug her perplexed gaze to mine. "Now, it's 98.6!"

Glory, hallelujah!

God had moved swiftly on our behalf. I couldn't help thinking what may have happened had I not obeyed His voice. The nurse summoned the doctor in excitement. When he bounded into the room, Teresa was seated on the side of the bed. It was like the man who demons had tormented, then was suddenly clothed and in his right mind. That was Teresa. The doctor was looking upon a woman who, minutes before, was inches from death but was now clothed and in her right mind.

The doctor couldn't explain how Teresa was suddenly able to communicate. "I don't know what happened, but I'm telling you she's going back into her former state and still won't fully recover," he said. "Her brain will not be fully restored, and she'll be a vegetable the rest of her life."

His words didn't pierce me in the least. "God has done the work," I said.

Teresa was given her discharge papers and a wheelchair for me to transport her in. Days before, these halls had been riddled with the cries of a woman on the verge of taking her last breath. Now, she was going home. And when the nurses and patients saw the woman who'd been confined behind the yellow tape, screaming the morbid cry of death and told she'd never recover, being rolled down the hall to return home, they began to applaud. It was a sweet, collective praise of victory. Teresa was a sign of hope and that God will forever have the final say.

Leaving the hospital that day, all of Teresa's ailments were left behind with the yellow tape that had been tossed in the trash. God performed a complete work. From that day forward, Teresa never experienced a relapse or had another fever. It was a complete recovery, and 30 years later, my wife is doing excellent. Healthy, strong, anointed, and as beautiful as ever. God is awesome!

Teresa's recovery from meningitis was the first true miracle I experienced God perform for my family, though there would be many other challenges we had to face. Remember, God told me I would be tried by fire to come out pure gold.

There was a time when my oldest daughter had a blood clot. Her nose bled so much her pillowcase would be covered in it every morning. We took her to the doctor, who informed us that she had "puffs" in her nose, which were the equivalent of ulcers. To alleviate the issue, her nose would have to be split open, and the ulcers would have to be cut out. The worst part was hearing that she'd have a scar on her nose for the rest of her life.

Here we go again, I thought. Disappointed, I did what I knew to do again – I prayed. And God told me He was going to heal her. So, we prayed and anointed her before telling the doctor we were trusting the Lord. Now I'm not calling the doctors hypocrites, but some doctors don't believe in the spiritual dynamics and the mysteries of God.

As they prepared for my daughter's surgery, another X-ray had to be taken before sedating her. The X-ray was taken that morning, and the doctors came to us holding both X-rays in shock. Where the previous one had shown the abnormalities, the new one was completely blank. There were no puffs! Another miracle! God healed my daughter, and her nose never bled again. God performed the surgery before the doctors had a chance to touch her. He proved yet again, not by might nor by power, but by His Spirit. He had healed her nose completely of blood disease. Today, Shaneri is 45 years old and has never had that problem again.

As I walked with the Lord and grew in spirit, my prayer life strengthened, and I learned how to trust Him more when situations began to arise. There was a time when Teresa was working at the Federal Reserve Bank. Her co-workers called me "Papa Bear" because I'd get her teddy bears in a cup as gifts, and everyone marveled at it. One co-worker in particular, Brenda, fell ill and was diagnosed with breast cancer. Doctors told her the cancer had spread, and there was basically nothing they could do. The staff called requesting I pray for Brenda, and I agreed.

I invited Brenda to come to our house in Rowlett. As soon as I opened the door to greet her, the fear in Brenda's eyes gripped my heart. "We're going to pray for you," I assured her.

Brenda's hair had been taken by chemotherapy. She removed the wig she was wearing, mortified that her hair was gone.

"We're not going to worry about that," I consoled her. "We're trusting God to do a miracle. Do you believe it?"

Brenda choked back tears with a nod. "I remember when Teresa had meningitis, and you prayed for her. When we saw Teresa come back, we knew God is a healer."

Because Brenda was already in agreement, I grabbed Teresa, we got the oil, anointed, and prayed for her. "God's going to heal you of this cancer." This was the first time I had ever prayed for someone with a terminal disease, but I felt the power of God surge through me.

Several days later, Brenda called me. She said her doctor called her in to perform emergency surgery on her breasts one more time. The cancer had spread from her breasts to her brain, and they needed to see what they were up against. Doctors told her she only had a short time, and it was crucial that they try again.

"What should I do?" Brenda asked.

I was confident in what God had shown me again. "Go ahead and let them do the surgery. When they open you up, they won't find any cancer."

"Okay, Papa. I'll do what you said." Brenda sounded more relieved than at the start of our conversation. I knew she was going to be fine; it sounded as if she did, too.

Five hours later (after performing the emergency surgery), I received a call from one of Brenda's relatives, hysterical and screaming on the phone.

"Slow down. Tell me what you're trying to say," I prodded.

I heard her take a deep breath before clearly blurting, "When the doctors opened Brenda, there was no cancer!"

I have to pause right here. Even now, recounting this testimony gives me chills. God had miraculously healed Brenda of all cancer! Not a trace of it was left in her body, none whatsoever. Brenda lived for 23 more years, but when she passed, it wasn't because of cancer, which never once returned. She died from a heart condition. True to His Word, God healed her of that dreadful disease.

During that time, I wasn't doing crusades or traveling the world. I was just doing the will of God wherever I could go. For three years, I prayed for nursing home residents and would receive testimonies from the ones I prayed for, declaring what God had done for them.

But I had my own testimony, too. I was working in shipping and receiving at Goodwill, making $2.85 an hour. While there, I had the opportunity to witness and minister to many of the patients who came through. One day I was in the back where I stayed to myself, reading my Word, and was approached by a Jewish man – a wealthy business owner, who'd come back there to check on his product.

"What are you reading?" he asked.

A smile spread across my face. "I'm reading the Bible." I held it up for him to see.

He looked from me to the book, curiosity in his eyes. "What part are you reading?"

"I'm reading about Jesus in the New Testament," I announced with pride.

The man's head bobbed from side to side. "Jesus is not real. He's nothing but a myth, a fable."

This challenge was the kind of opportunity I welcomed. Time to share the goodness of God. "Jesus is very real, and He's alive," I told him.

"Jesus isn't real. He's a fake and a fable," the man reiterated with more assertiveness.

I mustered the same conviction he had. "That may be your belief, but I believe in Him."

Three weeks later, a call came over the work intercom stating the man was there and wanted to see me. My heart pounded against my chest. *Why is he here to see me?*

This man was one of Goodwill's best clients. His request for me by name sent a shockwave through the building. Whatever it was he wanted, everyone figured it couldn't be good. One of my supervisors ran to the back where I was.

"What did you tell him, Roscoe?" he asked.

"Nothing," I said. "He asked me about the Bible, and I told him. That's all."

My supervisor's hands flew to his temples. "That's all? You probably offended him. If you did and we lose this contract, you're going to be fired!"

Oh, God. This was my only job, and I was barely making any money. I couldn't afford to lose this job. My family needed that money.

"You don't have to go up there; he's coming back here," the supervisor huffed.

I am in trouble...

I didn't have the opportunity to gather my thoughts before the man appeared in the doorway and walked over to me. He stood in front of me, briefly paused, then got down on both knees.

I was perplexed. "Sir, what are you doing?"

"I want you to pray for me, that I might know Jesus," he choked.

Without hesitation, I said, "I sure will. What may I pray for you?"

The man's head dropped. "My wife left me a couple of weeks ago and took my daughter with her. She wasn't happy with all my wealth, and our marriage was on the rocks." Tears streamed down his face. "I want you to pray to Jesus that my wife returns."

"I will pray for you that you come to know Jesus and that He will bring your wife back," I said.

Two days after I prayed for him, this man bolted inside the store, raced back to where I was working, and embraced me tightly. "I want you to know that the prayer you prayed for me worked! My wife came back to me with my daughter, and she tore up the divorce papers, just like you said! You don't realize what that has done for me!"

All I had done was what God prepared me for, to pray in the name of Jesus. Still, my heart was overjoyed that another soul had come to know Jesus.

"I want to hire you as my counselor," the man excitedly announced.

Surely I hadn't heard him right. "Sir? Your counselor?"

"Yes! I will hire you as a counselor and give you an office in my warehouse. You'll just sit in the office, and when I need counseling, you'll give it to me," he explained. "I'll pay you $25,000 to start."

In 1985, that salary was phenomenal! I was so excited. I broke into a happy dance. "Oh God, I thank You!"

I called Teresa and gave her the testimony. I couldn't wait to get home and thank God. While I did thank Him in the office, I wanted to get home, humble myself and get on my knees to thank Him properly for what He had done. I will always give Him glory, honor, and praise for blessing me in such phenomenal ways.

I got home and went straight into prayer. As I thanked Him for the blessing, God interrupted me.

You're not to take this job.

I went silent. "Lord, I don't understand."

You are not to take this job, God repeated. *I want you to call him back and tell him you're not taking the job. I want you to stay right where you are until I tell you to move.*

I broke down in tears. "Why would You leave me stuck here, making $2.85 an hour?"

I didn't put you here to make a lot of money. I put you there to be a witness unto Me and bring glory and praise to My name.

Like I always did and always will, I obeyed God. I've been walking with God for over 40 years, and at age 70, I will continue to obey God! He knows my heart and my desires. I called the gentleman and turned down the job offer, knowing it was the right thing to do because it was what God said.

"Think it over," he responded. "And if you ever change your mind, I'm still willing to do it."

I never did call him back.

A year later, everything was put behind me, and I still worked the same job. Many people there were disabled or had mental issues, but one man convinced me that he had received instructions from the devil himself to attack me. I'd known him a while and always addressed him in a nice, even tone. On this particular day, something was different with him.

I got him out of bed, and he scowled at me with venom. "What's your problem?" he spat.

"Nothing, man. How are you doing?" I responded in my usual friendly tone. Before I knew it, he pushed me, and I pushed him back. In seconds, he was punching me, escalating the situation into a full-blown tussle.

He kept punching me, then threw me on the ground and stomped me. The other patients were incoherent and didn't understand what was happening; their natural response was to laugh at me. Immediately, my mind reverted back to my old ways, and I thought about who I **used** to be. The fighter. The dude who sought revenge. It was about to be a straight knock-out.

Revenge is mine, I told myself.

I grabbed a metal pipe, ready to attack. Just as I moved to swing, the Holy Spirit told me, *Put that pipe down. You are not to attack him. Go in that bathroom, hug him, and tell him you love him and you forgive him.*

What!

"Forgive him? He beat me!" I argued.

Yes, he did, but you are to go in there, tell him you forgive him, and you love him.

Per usual, I obeyed the Lord. The pipe bounced against the floor as I released it from my hands, and I wandered into the bathroom. I grabbed the guy and hugged him. "I forgive you, and I love you."

The man's stiff posture melted in my arms. "I don't understand. Why? I'm the one who fought you. Why?"

"Because the Lord told me." I hugged him again. This time, he hugged me back.

One of my co-workers, a supervisor, also professed to be a Christian. She heard about the altercation and told me she didn't understand how I allowed this guy to beat me and do nothing about it. "If that had been me, I would've beat him back," she said.

"You don't understand. I couldn't do that. Because the Lord spoke to me and told me not to," I explained.

She was confused, so I shared with her about my encounters with the Holy Spirit and how I was striving to follow the ways of the Lord. Now, she professed to be a Christian, but when I told her my stance, she laughed in my face! Not only did she not believe in the Holy Spirit, she had the evidence of speaking of tongues but chose not to.

"That's the difference between you and me," I told her. "And that's why I couldn't defend myself."

She laughed at me again and told me I was crazy.

Five months later, God removed me from Goodwill after three years. I never got a raise or made above $2.85 for **three years**. It was like Jacob working for Laban without getting anything in return. Still, God was getting the glory out of my being there until He moved me from Goodwill to Parkside Drug Rehab Center.

Every Friday, we'd go up the street to Catfish Smith's, which was right up the street from my job. On one occasion, a young woman told me the restaurant belonged to her uncle. It had been at least five months since I'd seen her. I was standing in the back of the restaurant, looking at this young lady as she stared at me, both of us trying to recognize where we knew each other from. It was the Christian from Goodwill who'd laughed when I refused to fight the patient back. She looked familiar, but not the same as I was used to seeing her. There was a glow on her that hadn't been present before.

She spotted me, ran from behind the counter over to me, and pulled me in for a hug. "I'm so excited because I wanted to tell you what happened," she said.

"What happened?" I asked.

A huge grin spread across her face. "The day you told me why you didn't fight back and you left, I ended up getting fired because one of the patients jumped on me, and I decided to defend myself. We ended up fighting all over the plant."

She explained that although she'd been attacked, being that she was a supervisor and not mentally disabled like the patient, she was let go from her position.

"After that incident, I asked God what kept you from fighting, but not me. God told me, '*He had the Holy Ghost, and you don't have it*,'" she said.

After that, she went to the prayer chapel, got on her knees, and asked the Lord to give her what I have. He filled her with the Holy Ghost, and she began speaking in tongues. "You were right, and I want to thank you," she said.

It was another instance where God got glory from my actions and my lack of reaction. Often, many people I've prayed for (especially in my church) have been healed, marriages have been restored, and God has done so much more. He was showing me that I had a special gift of praying for people that manifested in healing.

Once my calling became even more apparent, I began traveling, doing the work as God instructed. In 2000, I went to Africa.

As I ministered in Africa, there was a long line that seemed to go on for miles. People with AIDS and other illnesses gathered for their healing. Now before this, Rob, a gentleman at Teresa's job, had contracted AIDS as well. He remembered my praying for Teresa when she had meningitis and the woman who had cancer. The doctors told Rob he wouldn't survive more than two more days, and he asked me to come to the hospital to pray for him.

Teresa and I went to Baylor Hospital to pray for Rob. His room was dark; the stench of impending death hovered in the air. He barely breathed through the oxygen tank he was connected to and all the other wires from the various machines. His partner was seated by his side, gloom hooding his eyes.

Rob had lost a massive amount of weight and was unconscious. I laid my hand across his toes, praying that God would heal him. When I was done, I scooted to his side and whispered in his ear. "When the Lord raises you up, don't you sin anymore."

Rob didn't respond. I just prayed. His family hugged me, and I left.

Several days later, Teresa's closest friend called her, astonished. "You won't believe this, but Rob is out of the hospital!"

God had worked a miracle again! God had raised him up, and he was back at work, telling all the people on the job how "Papa" prayed for him and he'd been healed. God did that!

There are so many testimonies I could share about how the power of God has healed people and raised people up, but there are too many to share in a single space. However, I will share one of the greatest miracles I have witnessed in my time. It was like Paul said, that thing I feared the most had come upon me.

I traveled to Zimbabwe in 2000 with one of my ministers and

my son. I prayed for an influx of patients, and I remember the pastor telling me, "You prayed for a woman who had AIDS. I want you to know that the same woman was bedridden and is now sitting up!"

"My God!" I exclaimed. "One day, I'm coming back here again. God has shown me He heals AIDS, and I'm going to come back and pray for a lot of people."

The Holy Spirit spoke to me that day. *You will come back, but you will have a greater testimony.*

"Yes, Lord," I replied, not fully comprehending that the saddest, most trying time of my faith and walk with God was impending. My wife had faced death, and I prayed for her. I prayed for my daughter, and God healed her of bleeding ulcers. I prayed for so many people who testified God had healed them, but it really came close this time.

My children mean the world to me. I love my son and daughters and would do anything for them. Nothing surpasses my love and compassion for Andre, Shaneri, and Kermitrice. Only my closest friends, relatives, the church, and pastors know the testimony I'm about to give.

In 2006, my family was living in Rowlett. Andre was extremely sick. He'd always been a stocky young man, weighing about 226 pounds. He was extremely healthy but had lost so much weight. When I took him to the doctor, he had dwindled down to 90 pounds – an over 100-pound weight loss. He had multiple dizzy spells and kept falling out. Even his complexion darkened way beyond his normal skin color.

Teresa and I rushed Andre to the emergency room at Rowlett Hospital. After running some tests, the doctor came to us and said, "Your son's sicker than you can imagine, but because of the law, I'm unable to disclose his medical records since he's over the age of 16."

Naturally, I was upset because I wanted to know what was happening to my son! The doctor advised that she would send the records to Andre's doctor to disclose his condition. Teresa and I took him back home and helped him back to bed. He was so skinny, so frail – this was not the vibrant, healthy Andre we knew.

The next day, I took Andre to Dr. Steven Chase, my doctor of over 34 years. Dr. Chase knew the medical history of my entire family, including Andre, who was 25 years old. Andre got completely undressed, and my heart sank. He was a near skeleton. He looked malnourished like he hadn't eaten in months. Skin and bones. I couldn't believe what I was seeing. This couldn't be my son.

Dr. Chase had received the records from the emergency room but advised me he would run some tests of his own and would disclose the results as soon as he had them. He asked Andre a series of questions, ran the tests, and we went back home.

The next day, Dr. Chase called, saying he needed me to bring Andre back to his office. The news he had to deliver shouldn't be delivered on the phone, so he needed to see us in person. I knew something was drastically wrong. When we got to the office, Dr. Chase's face was somber.

"I don't know how to tell you this," he said, "but I have to tell you what we've diagnosed."

This is my son, Andre – the only son I have. As much as I desperately wanted to hear some good news, Dr. Chase's melancholy voice and cloud cast over his face said to expect the worst.

"Andre has AIDS, in the worst stage." Surely I hadn't heard him right. But as he continued, I knew I had heard correctly. "We've looked into his X-rays and bloodstream. If his CB4 (blood count) were 500, I would think he would have more longevity, a little longer time to live – maybe a year or two. But his CB4 is 12…"

That's right. I said 12.

Andre didn't even have an immune system anymore. The disease had devoured his entire immune system. Everything went blank as Dr. Chase told me and my son that he had between four days and a week to live. Andre screamed; I almost collapsed.

"Dad, I don't want to die!" Andre shrieked.

"God, why!" I hollered. "Why me? Why my son?"

I called Teresa and delivered the news, then told my daughters. It was like terror had overtaken our home, everyone screaming and crying. The entire house was in mourning, from my son-in-law to my daughter and wife.

"Daddy, don't let me die!" Andre wailed.

In my mind, I wondered, *What can I do? I'm not God. I can't do anything. I'm just like you!*

What do you do when the doctor tells you your only son has no more than a week to live? How do you deal with it? I had never faced anything like this in my life. My wife had been near death, yes. But this is almost 20 years later. *God, give me the strength.* I silently prayed.

I was pastoring during this time, and the congregation I pastored was clueless about our devastating news. They knew Andre was sick but were unaware of the diagnosis. How does a pastor tell his church members that his son, the choir director, is about to die within days? I had to do something. They needed to know. I told

Teresa we had nothing else to do but pray. Prayer was my greatest weapon, the best line of defense against this cruel diagnosis. My connection to the Word was through prayer.

So, I went to God in prayer. "Lord, this is my only seed. I have no other seed who can carry on my name." I spoke to God like I'm speaking to you. "God, I'm asking in Jesus' name that You would intervene and step in and heal him. I know You're a healer. You healed my wife. Lord, heal my son."

God didn't speak to me right then and there, so I went on as if things were normal. We lived 25 miles outside the church, and I cried all the way down the highway there. Before I pulled into the parking lot, I'd pull over and dry my tears because I didn't want anyone at the church to know what was happening. When someone asked how I was doing, my answer was always the same: "Everything's going fine."

Eventually, I knew I would have to let the church in on what was happening. The last thing I wanted was for Andre to die suddenly without preparing them first. Besides, my family and I were already going through enough trauma to deal with the added stress.

One night, God spoke to me in my sleep. *I'm going to heal him.*

The sound of His voice jolted me awake. "You're going to heal him, Lord?"

Yes. This is what I want you to do. I want you to take Andre and stand him before the congregation. And I want you to get the report that says he has AIDS. Take the report and lift it before the congregation and anoint it with oil, He said. *And I want you to curse this report. And when you curse the report, I'm going to reverse the curse that has come upon him, and I will not let him pass through death. I will raise him up.*

Jesus!

I told Andre what God said to me. "Dad," he said, "I want to go. I know God's going to heal me."

God gave me a scripture – Psalm 136: *"You shall not die, but you shall live so you can declare the goodness of the Lord in the land of the living."*

We brought Andre to church, where I finally shared what was happening with the congregation. Everyone started screaming, just as we had before this. They screamed and hollered like the world was ending. There was so much commotion. I had to yell, "Stop! Listen to me. We're going to see a miracle happen here. I want you to trust me."

I stood Andre before the congregation, took the report I had anointed, prayed, and cursed that report in the name of Jesus. Then I laid hands on Andre, and he fell out. After he fell out, I took him to Peabody Clinic – an AIDS clinic in Dallas. The doctor there administered a physical, and when he came back, he said, "Somebody in this family must be a minister."

"Why do you say that?" I asked.

The doctor glanced at Andre's paperwork, astonished. "I checked your son's organs, and none of his major organs are in bad condition. His heart is working just fine, his lungs are good, his kidneys are good. There's no sign of hepatitis or anything in his body. Somebody has to be praying!"

I told him I was a pastor – a praying pastor who'd been praying for my son.

"It worked," the doctor told me, "because God is doing something."

Andre had been so sick; his tongue was decomposing in his

mouth. He showed Teresa and me, and it was horrible to look at, but he is my son. God began to show his hand.

Two weeks later, I returned to the Peabody Clinic with Andre to have more tests run. Over 100,000 bacteria were fighting against him the last time we were there. Now, that number has dwindled to 45,000! Eighteen years ago, God healed my son of AIDS. He was back on his feet, he's still preaching today, and we rejoice in God. My church and everyone who knows us cried and shouted, giving Him the glory for working another miracle. Andre has gone on to his own prophetic ministry, praying for people who receive their healing.

This is what God can do for you. My son was healed from AIDS. People were healed of so many things, and I can testify to God's miracle-working power. That's why this book is titled, *Coming Out of the Fire*, because I've seen God bring me out of the fire, and I've seen the results of faith in action. As you read this book, I want you to believe. Our God is an awesome God, in Jesus' name!

CHAPTER Eight

If I Could Just Tell My Story

"And my God will supply every need of yours according to his riches in glory in Christ Jesus."

~ Philippians 4:19, ESV

This final chapter is the best part of my life. One thing that God said that has stayed with me and will stay with me all of my life until the Lord calls me home is *Many are called, few are chosen. I chose you; you didn't choose Me. I have ordained you, and I have anointed you to teach and preach the gospel. Lo and behold, many shall come against you, but if I be for you, I'm more than the world against you. But thou are not ready. But after I've tried you through the fire, thou shall come forth as pure gold.*

I didn't know the fire God was talking about, especially because He told me this just a couple of months into my walk with Him. The more I walked with God, the more I began to understand the fire, tribulations, and trials I would have to endure to be a mature believer and minister of the gospel.

I remember the days of being young, teaching, preaching, and witnessing the signs and wonders of God. One thing I don't want to forget to mention is that I was in an organization years ago, Church of the Living God. I loved it, and it was a wonderful organization. The presiding pastor, Bishop Wallace, was a great woman of God, and I was installed as the district elder over the state of Mississippi, where I presided over six churches. Mississippi was a part of my maturity and integral in launching my ministry.

I can't overlook that I spent 16 years at Heartline Ministry when I first began serving. We were first called Calvary Temple under Bishop Clifford Frazier, a great Man of God whom I still consider my bishop and the only father I ever had. I have and will continue to honor him. Calvary Temple landed on Military Parkway in the Pleasant Grove area of Dallas before migrating to Buckner Avenue in the same area. Ministry life at Calvary Temple was tremendous! Bishop Frazier taught me everything I know in ministry. He was very instrumental in teaching me how to be a good Man of God and a man of integrity who would hammer the Word of God and discipline correctly. But the Lord directed me to return to Oak Cliff because I had unfinished work to complete. I had an idea what He was talking about, but I obeyed the Lord.

I didn't want to return to Oak Cliff because I was happy where I was. Who wouldn't be filled with joy to serve in a ministry that served and chased after God the way Calvary Temple did? This was my family; 16 years brought us close together, and I couldn't imagine being torn from the people I loved and my spiritual father. I felt like leaving would separate me from my pastor and the friends I'd made, but the Lord will call you out, just like He called Moses out. Remember, Moses was brought out of the Nile River, and God called him to go back to Egypt, just as He called me to go back to Oak Cliff.

Back in Oak Cliff, our ministry Alpha and Omega Ministries started in a shopping center with four people: my wife, Teresa, Evangelist Waters, and her mother, Mother Waters. Together, the four of us started what would eventually become a legacy for the Kingdom. Later, my sister, Elder Karlene Sneed (who is still a member of my church), and Karlene's daughter, Evangelist Sharon Lee (also still a member), also added to the ministry. We praised, taught, learned, got healed, delivered, and set so many things in that shopping center. Taking care of God's business, as He took care of us. I'll never forget those days.

Thirty years before this, my bishop, other members, and I walked on the same land when I was simply Brother Williams. Five years into launching the ministry, I never would have dreamed that God would bless us to move from that small storefront location to build the church where we currently reside on that very land! My pastor claimed this land would be where he would build his church, but it wasn't constructed while we were members. Who would have thought that all these years later, God would bring me to build on that same land? It was and is still a mystery to me. But God sent me there, and with the help of the members, my beloved wife, whom I love and cherish, and my children, who have been a support to my ministry all my life, along with my family, brothers, sisters, and friends, we built this church – together.

We built a 13,000-square-foot church, and God blessed us tremendously to grow. After five years, God told me again to build. So we stepped out on His command and constructed a 24,000-square-foot multi-purpose facility on the same land as the church. God has blessed us to have a 42,000-square-foot building with a full gymnasium and daycare. We have a partnership with one of the largest districts in our area, serving pre-k students, as well as various ministries that pour from the main Alpha and Omega infrastructure.

I wanted to call this book, *Coming Out of the Fire* because of the insurmountable trials, miracles, wonders, and blessings we have experienced from day one. Even the man who gave us the land – it seemed implausible, but God specializes in the impossible! Mr. Gregory said places were available to build in Oak Cliff, but I was adamant because God told me to build right there.

I drove to Ellis County to meet with Mr. Gregory and was taken aback by how nice he was. We had a good meeting, and when I left, he rang my phone.

"I don't believe in God. I'm not a believer," he said. "But I believe in what you're saying, and I want to help you."

God had touched this man's heart who didn't even recognize or believe in Him in such a miraculous way! Only He can move the heart of those who don't honor His power! Let me paint this picture for you so you can truly understand what happened here. Mr. Gregory sold us the land for the same price he'd purchased it for ten years ago during the savings and loans bust that had rocked Texas! A little under two acres of land, right off a major freeway.

Keep reading because it gets better!

Before he met us, Mr. Gregory bought the land for $54,000; he sold it to us for that same price, with no interest or anything! Somebody needs to shout right there!

The blessings hadn't stopped there. Of course, now we needed a building, but construction was foreign to me. Mr. Gregory took me under his wing and introduced me to the bank's vice president. Remember, God told me if He was for me, no one could be against me, not even a man who didn't believe in Him. I didn't have credit. The church didn't have credit. We didn't even have members who had the credit we needed. Not even a building fund to help us. But God sent a secret weapon to work on our behalf – Mr. Gregory, who served as a buffer between the vice president of the bank, Susan Wilson, and me.

"What are you going to do with this money, Mr. Williams?" Ms. Wilson's voice was stern.

My confident posture belied how I was shaking inside. "We're going to build a church."

Ms. Wilson's brows rose. "How much money do you have in the bank?"

"None."

"How many members do you have?"

"25."

She fired off so many questions my head spun. I'm not sure if I was sweating, but the room was scorching. I was facing a giant, but I knew I had Jesus on my side.

"You have no money, no members; how do you expect us to give you a loan?" Ms. Wilson asked.

If I'd never been sure of anything, I was confident in the power of my God. "I'm just trusting God."

Ms. Wilson eyed me with a heavy sigh. "I'm sorry, we're not going to be able to help you. We just don't loan money to give away."

"I understand," I said as I walked away.

I may have walked off without the loan, but it wasn't in defeat. I want you to know that if God is in the midst of what you're going through, and if He has orchestrated the situation or circumstance, it will come to pass! His Word will not go out void.

Seven days later, I received a call from Ms. Wilson. "Preacher, I don't know you, but I believe you're determined to build this church. I believe God is with you, and I'm going to approve this loan."

Here I am with the audacity to apply for any loan, let alone one of this magnitude, with no credit or collateral. I had nothing, and this woman turned around, told me she was approving my loan, and gave me a check for $500,000!

Read that again – $500,000!

"I'm giving you this to build your church," she said.

GLORY!

We wasted no time securing an architect, and God even gave us favor with them. The build for this church should have been $1 million, but we were working with brothers in the Lord. And our brothers built the church for $500,000. No one can do that but God! I thank God for Brother Timothy and Brother Charles, and I thank them for what they did for us. I can never forget it.

We didn't have much land to work with, so Charles suggested we build "up." We started off constructing a metal building, but the price of steel went up and out the roof! We couldn't afford it, but I had already ordered a pile of it to come in from Pompano Beach, Florida. I had to call the owner of Coastal Steel and tell him we couldn't afford to continue the build because the steel's price was skyrocketing the way it had. We changed the infrastructure to wood and went on with that. Nothing was going to get in our way.

I wish you could hear the excitement in my voice right now. This final chapter is so powerful I can hardly contain myself enough to get it written! My heart is leaping with joy, and I hope yours is, too!

So, we'd been in the building for five years, with 22-foot walls, with the intention of a remodel later on down the line. It seemed like a waste of money to me, but our builders knew what they were doing, and I trusted them. Out of nowhere, on December 23, 2003, the owner of Coastal Steel contacted me.

"I remember you and that you wanted to build a church one day," he said.

Naturally, this close to Christmas, I assumed this was a spam call but decided to entertain him for a moment. "Yes, sir, but who are you?"

He repeated his name and reiterated that he was the owner of Coastal Steel. "I was sitting in my office, and your name came to my mind," he said. "I heard it spoken to me, so I called you. I want to be a blessing to you."

I was waiting for the punchline because this had to be a joke, a fraud, something.

"I have this building I built for a gentleman who wanted a bigger building," he continued. "We built him a larger facility, but now we have this building up here that we're not doing anything with. I want to tell you that we have this building that will be 90 x 70 feet."

I drew in a breath and exhaled. "How much are you asking for this building?"

"I'm only asking you to pay what I put into the building. I'm not charging you anything else."

So, I'm quickly calculating in my mind that this will cost me at least $400,000 because of the size of the building and the cost of steel. But to my amazement, the gentleman had another number in mind.

"I'm asking for $59,000."

"There's gotta be something wrong," I blurted.

The gentleman's amused chuckle sailed through the line. "I remember you wanting that gym, and I want you to have this."

I didn't want to turn it down, but a major concern ate at me. "Our walls are only 22 feet. I'm not sure we can accommodate the size."

"Sure you can," he said. "Our walls are only eight feet tall. But I want to help you. I will have my architects rework the plans, make those rafters to be 22 feet, and I won't charge you anything for it. I'll also make sure to build a roof, put four doors on it, and install windows at no cost."

I couldn't believe how God was moving! This couldn't be true! All he was asking was $5,000 to hold the building, and the rest could be paid out. I was cautious, thinking that it could still be a fraud. It just sounded so "good." Still, I needed to check him out.

I asked again where he was located, and he assured me he was in Pompano Beach. A good friend of mine was out that way, so I contacted him and asked if he'd ever heard of the guy. My friend said yes indeed, he'd heard of Coastal Steel and that the company had been there for 45 years.

"It can't be a fraud," my friend told me.

Without hesitation, I jumped into action. I only had $2,000 to put towards it, so if this was going to happen, I needed help. First, I called my daughter to ask how much she could loan me towards the down payment. By the grace of God, she had $3,000 and agreed to loan it to me.

I called Coastal Steel's owner back, Fed-Ex'd the money to him, and he sent a contract back. Then, the bank issued a second loan, and we brought the building from Florida to Texas. That's how the facility came to be. Sometimes the mountains don't seem so big when God pushes them out of the way, not even building a 26,000-square-foot facility. I'm telling you, a quote for $3 million from one gentleman was shrunk to a $5,000 down payment, all because of the hand of God!

We started the process intending to build a little at a time, but the contractor said it was too much on him and eventually stepped away from the project. But God spoke to me and told me, *You'll be the contractor. I will tell you how to read the plans, and you'll tell the men.*

God told me exactly what to say and do, and we watched as favor went to work again. Valued at $3.5 million, we built the facility for $1.8 million! Jesus, hallelujah! Thank You, Jesus! We did that by the grace of God. The gymnasium and the classrooms – all built by the goodness of God's grace. God has blessed and continues to bless our ministry.

Two gentlemen, Deacon Curtis Nash, and Minister Peter Lee, also played a hand in showing how God's hand moved in the ministry that I must share with you. We'd gone down to Mississippi, where I was preaching a five-day revival at various churches. One particular night, there was an incident in Ft. Worth, Texas, where a man had broken into a church and killed some young people. I was so upset when I received the news. I said the devil is a lie!

In the midst of tragedy, an anointing came upon me like never before. I'd never seen the power of God like this. Fifty people. *Fifty people.* No one laid hands on them. There wasn't prayer or an altar call, I just preached, and the Holy Ghost fell upon that church! People were rolling on the floor. The ushers fell down, and people everywhere were speaking in tongues. Suddenly, people flooded the altar, throwing their glasses, drugs, cigarettes, and all these things on the altar. They were being delivered, and it was an incredible sight to see. So phenomenal, so amazing! Fifty people received the Holy Ghost, all at the same time, almost like the Day of Pentecost! The way God moved was completely mind-blowing, and He wasn't done yet.

The next night, I was preaching, and two young ladies approached me – one a Muslim, the other a Jehovah's Witness. They asked me how to get the Holy Ghost and serve the Lord. I put two chairs in the front of the congregation and sat them back-to-back, with instructions to just listen while I preached. As I preached, both ladies received the Holy Ghost and bolted from their chairs, speaking in tongues. Revival hit that house in a whole new way! The Spirit of God moved so mightily. It was astonishing. I'll never get tired of watching His power work.

God was blessing us tremendously through the work of preaching and revivals, but He also began blessing us financially, too. In 2002, the Lord spoke to me. *I'm going to bless you with the blessings of Abraham. And when I bless you, I want you to bless My people. When you bless My people, blessings will continuously come back to you. Remember what I said.*

Following the Word of the Lord, I began sowing into people's lives. Teresa and I were early in the ministry and sold our small, wooden frame house in Missouri to a neighbor. In the meantime, we applied for a beautiful 3,500-square-foot brick home in Rowlett. It was an elegant, two-story house with a pool and all the luxury amenities. After applying for the house, the owner told us she would let us rent it and tried to improve our credit to qualify to buy it.

As we went through the process, so many things came crashing down on us. First, Teresa was involved in a brutal car accident. Then, I was working on the windows, 30 feet in the air, by myself. I should have had my son with me, but I didn't have the patience to wait on him. I figured I could get it done by myself. Well, the ladder slipped, and I crashed down to the concrete patio.

Crack!

The sound of my foot breaking rang in my ears. It was the most agonizing pain I'd ever felt! I crawled to the door, full of paint, in excruciating pain. Teresa was in a back brace, and couldn't physically help me, so I called for help and was taken to Medical City. My goodness, my foot was swollen five times bigger than its normal size! I was told it was a bad sprain; however, the next day, I got a call from the hospital saying I needed to come in for emergency surgery. My left calcaneus (the heel bone) had cracked into five pieces and was shattered.

I rushed in for the surgery and ended up having pins put in my foot all the way to my toes. I was out of work for a year and a half! I was in a hard cast for six months, then a boot for six more, and had to learn to walk on crutches. Disabled, surviving off a disability check, and unemployed. There was no way we were going to qualify for the house. I was totally devastated.

God began to work so mightily through this, showing just how we were going to come out of the fire. At the time, this house was selling for $254,000. We didn't have the money, but God told me He would show me how He blesses. God moved on everyone who was involved with this house. First, the owner of the home was extremely wealthy. She wanted to be a blessing to us and took the house down to $111,000. The VA would loan us $90,000; however, we had to have $11,000 on our own to put with it.

I'd been unemployed for a year and a half, and we didn't have the money. I called the woman and told her we didn't have the money.

"I'm listening to your voice. You sound like a preacher," she said.

"I am," I told her.

"What faith are you?"

"I'm Pentecostal, ma'am."

"Really?" she chuckled. "I'm Pentecostal, too. My father always taught me if God blesses you, don't forget to bless others. I always want to be a blessing to the Man of God. How much money do you need?"

"$11,000," I told her.

"Alright, then I'm going to give you $11,000," she said.

Now this I couldn't believe. "Are you sure?"

"I'm going to give you the money, and you don't have to pay it back," she said. "I want to be a blessing to you. Expect a package from FedEx tomorrow."

Sure enough, the next day, there was a knock on the door, and when I opened it, the delivery man from FedEx was standing there with an envelope for me. I couldn't wait to snatch that package open! Just as she promised, I found a cashier's check for $11,000 inside with a note saying, "Do not give it back!" When I tell you God had been working things out, He really was. He's done so much. The title of this book could have been *Rags to Riches*.

God took our finances to a whole new level. We stayed in Rowlett, and I opened a successful energy-efficiency business, which is still thriving today. God blessed me and my family so much financially. We've been able to get out of debt, live in a nice home, have secured houses and land, and eventually, other properties. In the midst of all this, a prophetess told us God wanted to put us in a bigger house because Teresa and I love to do hospitality. I didn't think we needed a bigger house. I'd been content with the house that I had. But she insisted that God wanted us to have a bigger house.

"But I don't need a bigger house," I said.

"It's not what you need. It's what God wants to give you."

So, my daughter was out in DeSoto (where I live now) and was driving around when a brand new house being built caught her eye. She called and told me, "Daddy, I saw a house, and I know you'll love it. This is the house God wants you to have."

"I have to go see it then," I told her.

I drove out to DeSoto with my daughter and realtor, and I was stunned when I saw the house. Even before the car stopped, I was in love. I jumped out of the car while it was moving! "That's it, that's the house!"

We live in that house now. Five thousand square feet, two stories. God gave us favor with our home. We acquired it during a time of depression when the economy failed in 2007. Homes were up for foreclosure everywhere, yet we were buying. The asking price for this home was $500,000. The builder asked how much money I would be willing to put down because if I put down a certain amount, he would drop the price to $360,000.

God's grace came through again when I had the $30,000 to put down on the house with no problem. That was 13 years ago; Teresa and I are still there. The house was just the beginning. God started blessing even more and more.

Now back when I was ten years old, God gave me a vision. I drew a picture of a man (myself) with a wife and three or four kids. In the picture, we were walking on a property that we owned. I kept that picture in my heart, even as a child who wasn't saved. But I knew I wanted to build a big house on some land for my family, a house we could go to in the country. I went down to Jefferson (in east Texas) and purchased 78 acres of land there. My family and I are building an 8,000-square-foot ranch house, which will be complete in the next five months! Seven bedrooms, a living room, all the amenities, and we're going to put a pond on the land where we'll have our own fishing pond and our own swimming pool connected to the back. We're also installing our own basketball courts, a mini-golf course, and more, all on this massive blessing from God.

Because this is the final chapter of *Coming Out of the Fire*, I'm just talking about the blessings of God. He has blessed us in such a way that my three children have their own homes between Duncanville and DeSoto. We also have a family business, the Second-Step Daycare Learning Center offering pre-k classes, which is thriving. My children left very lucrative corporate jobs to work for our business and have succeeded. Each of us plays an integral part in running the businesses, and I pray this will be a lasting legacy for my children.

God has blessed Teresa and me with blessings, to be blessings. We have blessed people with cars and sown a tremendous amount of money into people, and those blessings have returned to us 1,000-fold. My wife drives a Mercedes. I have a Porsche, a BMW, a Silverado, a Mustang – I have cars I don't even need. I've given away mink coats and so many other things straight from my heart. I'm telling you, God will do just what He says! He will bless you abundantly, and we see God's prosperity continually blessing our lives.

We've traveled all around the world, Africa, Japan, Asia, Rome, Paris, and Jamaica – just a few of the places we've visited. In fact, Teresa, my sister, and I are preparing to head for Cape Town, South Africa, in June of 2023 for the fourth time. God has made provision for us where we are walking in prosperity. I'm honored to pastor a thriving church with wonderful people! I have some of the best members you could ever have, and I love them and what God is doing for us. We're active in our community. We sow and give back, blessing people over and over again. But it hasn't been without a cost.

I had to pay the price. I had to go through the fire, but coming out, it's impossible to count the numerous miracles and amazing things God has done for me. When my foot was broken, they said I'd never be able to wear a shoe again. God worked that miracle! I went to put my shoe on and kept saying, *Jesus, Jesus, Jesus!* As I praised, my foot slipped back into the shoe.

I've said it once, and I'll say it again, God works tremendous miracles, and I've seen it for myself. Even this year, I was diagnosed with prostate cancer, which no one in my family has ever had on either side. I wasn't stunned by the news because God had given me a dream that I was going to go through the fire yet one more time, but He would sustain me.

The doctors took X-rays and performed a bone scan, which the technician told me showed signs of metastatic cancer in my bones. I prayed to God and had another X-ray taken. This time, the techs claimed that I had cancer in my hip. Thank God that wasn't the case! Through my doctors' recommendations, surgery was required to remove the prostate, but the doctors turned around and gave me another PSA test. Initially, my PSA was at 31. Now, it was 0.023.

"There's nothing else in your body," my doctor informed me.

Praise God once again for the mighty works He has done!

I was supposed to have been in the hospital for seven days but spent one day there. I was supposed to have been off my feet for two months. How about I was back on my feet in four days? I'm here now, praising and telling you how good God really is! I resigned from the pulpit for two months but only spent two weeks away. I went right back to preaching, and I'm preaching right now to the glory of God.

I can talk all day about how God has blessed me and how He can and will bless you. I have one more testimony to leave you with.

Our taxes were really messed up. My financial person did them wrong, and we ended up owing hundreds of thousands of dollars to the IRS. Once you get in a rut with the IRS, you can't get out. But I'm a discerning Man of God. I knew the devil was setting it up to try and take away everything God had given me. I was paying money - BIG money, to settle the debt I owed. Once, I sent in a check for $85,000 because the IRS agents advised me the debt had accrued compounded interest. With interest, my bill ran up to...

$623,000!

That's how much the IRS told me I owed them. Each year, I was paying this large sum of money while trying to reach a settlement or feasible compromise to keep from losing everything. Because I made too much money, my offers were rejected. Keep in mind I was paying, but then the harassing letters started to come, threatening liens and the like. Eventually, my case was turned over to an agent who reviewed my records.

"I've found that you've given all your money to the church over the years," the agent said. "I'm going to take your money. I'm going to take your cars and your land. I'm putting a levy on everything! You've given all your money to God and the church. Let the church bail you out."

The agent filed charges and scheduled me to go to federal court. But the God who told me I would go through the fire and come out as pure gold, the God who told me that if I be for you, I'm more than the world against you, the God who told me I'm going to bless you and when I bless you, no man will be able to take you down, that God was who I went to.

I went back to my CPA (a different one than the one who had gotten me into this mess), and he told me he didn't know what to do. He hadn't managed to get me out of this trouble, and the flames were burning HOT. After praying, I found some people who said they knew something that could help. It wouldn't absolve me of the situation, but maybe I could get some relief. If anything, I'd still have to pay at least half or most of the money I owed.

After consulting with the others, I took the threatening letter from the IRS, anointed it, and prayed over it. I lifted the piece of paper unto the Lord. "God, You see where I'm at. You know what I've done and everything I've given to the church. I gave it out of obedience to be a good steward over Your inheritance. Lord, the devil is trying to come and take what You gave me! I'm trusting You."

I'm going to prove to you that no man can take you down, God said. And I'm going to show you that if I am for you, who can be against you.

After I came out of prayer, I had a renewed confidence that God was going to work it out, and I left it right there where I prayed. I'm here to testify that I received an email from the IRS about five days later (this is in writing, and I have it stored in my safe).

> **After careful consideration, we have decided to write off your debt of $623,000. Your balance is 0.**

I must have shouted, then grabbed Teresa and shouted some more! I was sent a certified letter confirming the debt had been canceled. God touched their hearts and wrote it off. GLORY!

We serve a miracle-working God. He can bless you in such a way that no one can stop it! How many people in my status do you know that have three-quarters of a million dollars written off without paying a dime after they've levied and threatened you? No matter the circumstance, you hold on and don't let the devil take you down!

In closing, I praise God, and I'm walking in the blessings and prosperity of God. If God be for you, who can be against you?

I hope you'll be inspired, touched, and read and believe these testimonies because God is no respecter of persons. I pray that God will bless you and that whatever you need, I pray you receive in Jesus' name. As the prophets have prophesied, I pray this book will touch people all over the world and draw them closer to God. I pray that God will get all the praise, all the glory, and all the honor, and I thank Him for these things; in Jesus' name, I pray, amen.

May the Lord bless you!

www.ingramcontent.com/pod-product-compliance
Lightning Source LLC
Chambersburg PA
CBHW020339010526
44119CB00035B/453/J